CHILD
CUSTODY
EVALUATIONS

CHILD CUSTODY EVALUATIONS

A PRACTICAL GUIDE

Dianne Skafte

SAGE PUBLICATIONS
The International Professional Publishers
Newbury Park   London   New Delhi

For information address:

SAGE Publications, Inc.
2455 Teller Road
Newbury Park, California 91320

SAGE Publications Ltd.
6 Bonhill Street
London EC2A 4PU
United Kingdom

SAGE Publications India Pvt. Ltd.
M-32 Market
Greater Kailash I
New Delhi 110 048 India

Printed in the United States of America

Library of Congress Cataloging in Publication Data

Skafte, Dianne.
    Child custody evaluations.

    1. Custody of children—United States. 2. Forensic
psychiatry—United States. I. Title.
KF547.S58   1985   346.7301'7   84-27637
ISBN 0-8039-2436-4   347.30617
ISBN 0-8039-2437-2 (pbk.)

93 94 10 9 8 7 6 5 4

CONTENTS

Acknowledgments

I will always be indebted to Ms. Mary Monroe, Ms. Flo Whinery, and the Family Court Services staff in Dallas, Texas, where I received my original training in child custody. Many of the approaches in this manual are direct legacies from them. Dr. Lanning Schiller has contributed ideas to the chapters on working with families and children. The discussion on visitation draws upon an article authored by Dr. William Wittlin and myself. Finally, my long and happy association with Dr. Doris Thomas has influenced my work in a positive way.

Introduction

This manual is dedicated to the custody evaluator who wants to do the best job possible under adverse circumstances. Why adverse? First, we are encountering people at one of the darkest times of their lives, when violent feelings of rage, despair, fear, and greed have been unleashed. We are not coming to them as therapists with healing words, but as evaluators with the power to wrench their children away from them. At least that is how they usually see it. Second, the task before us is formidable. We are to enter the tightly interwoven (though now torn) tapestry of a family system, identify the main supporting threads, understand how the children fit into the picture, and make predictions about how the various parts will unravel and reshape themselves over time. We are to express our findings, not in the form of a complex piece of literature that does justice to the holistic reality of this family, but in a brief report that makes skeletal analysis and either-or judgments. We are to do all of this in less than twenty hours of evaluation time.

Third and most important, we are operating in a context that has failure built into it. The legal structure was never designed to deal with subtle interpersonal issues such as how children should relate to each parent after divorce. Yet this is what it presumes to do when it makes a custody decision. We get the feeling that the legal process can only slice the tapestry into more fragments. We suspect that many families would not have ended up on the court docket if mediation or therapeutic assistance had been encouraged in the early stages. This discomfort with the system evokes a feeling of "all is not well" in our work, no matter how extraordinarily we perform our tasks.

Because of these factors, custody evaluation work never feels "easy," even after years of experience. It is assumed that anyone using this manual has a firm grounding in family therapy or casework already. The approaches and techniques outlined are appropriate only in the context of therapeutic experience, particularly with children. The practitioner is also advised to have access to a supervisor or staff trained in child custody. I know of no one who could launch out and do a responsible evaluation without this support.

Over the years I searched for a remedy to combat the perpetual heaviness of custody work. Finally I found it: writing secret reports. These were not the reports that one is required to write for the court. They were private documents that recorded thoughts unfit for judges or attorneys. I share one here, not because it deserves a place in posterity, but because it pays tribute to the frustrations that await every custody evaluator.

CUSTODY EVALUATION REPORT
RE: Dufus vs. Dufus

Children in Question:
Peachy, aged 6 and Bud, aged 10

At the order of the District Court of Boulder County, a custody evaluation was carried out by Dianne Skafte, who still regrets having met this family. Mr. Dufus, in his initial interview, clearly had difficulty focusing on the needs of the children. He resisted all attempts of the evaluator to discuss the children's future living arrangements. He also refused to be diverted from recounting in minute detail the discovery of Ms. Dufus in bed with the Fire Marshall. His general ability to assess the needs of young children and to provide guidance as a single parent is seriously questioned by this evaluator.

The initial interview with Ms. Dufus was equally unfruitful. The evaluator learned a great deal about the latest complications in *The Guiding Light* and took some notes on firefighting. But no information came to light about why either of these parents wanted custody of Peachy and Bud.

The visits to each parent's home were dark clouds in an otherwise unpleasant week. The evaluator's slacks were grease-stained, probably permanently, by sitting on a handful of old french fries that had been wedged into a corner of the sofa. A glass of Coke was declined after Bud was observed guzzling straight from the liter bottle.

After careful consideration of all the information gathered in this evaluation, no custody recommendation is offered. Whatever decision the court makes, it will have no effect on the Dufus family. In either household, the children will continue to sit blank-faced before the television, abuse the cat, and learn new facets of interpersonal destructiveness. Each parent will remarry within a year without having devoted the least thought as to why their first relationship failed. It is likely that their new partners will bring with them children of their own, creating new complexities for the court to sort through when the second round of divorces takes place. By then, this evaluator hopes to be in Fiji.

> Respectfully submitted,
> Custody evaluator

It should not be assumed from this pessimistic document that custody work is entirely gloomy. On the positive side is our awareness that we are contributing our skill and our compassion to solving difficult human problems. Although it is far from perfect, court resolution is the only option left for some families. Our mental health input brings a higher level of understanding and decision making to a legal process that urgently needs it. After all of our data have been collected and all of our skill brought to bear, we sometimes still find ourselves grappling with the unbelievably complex issue of what will be best for a child. How frightening it is to realize that judges make these same decisions daily with little psychological background and only a few hours of highly edited testimony to guide them.

In addition, there are unexpected personal rewards. The experience of all of those life stories settle down in one, like layers of humus, making the depths richer than before. In my mind I have sometimes thanked individuals for what they have taught me about the world. I have been face to face with realities that I would never have encountered in my own life. Despite its sadness, there is probably no work that is more meaningful. If one wants to make a difference in the world, this is a place to do it.

1

Setting the Stage

Those miserable, entangling evaluations that we hear about almost always began improperly. In most instances, the practitioner never established a proper framework for undertaking the case. A typical scenario is this:

An attorney calls the mental health professional to refer a client for assessment and perhaps therapy. This client, a woman, is involved in custody litigation. Shortly after she separated from her husband, he filed for divorce and asked for custody of their five-year-old daughter. The hearing date is a month away. This is a wonderful woman, the lawyer goes on to say, a good mother who loves her child. But the husband is alleging that she is a terrible mother and that the girl has emotional problems as a result. What the attorney requests is simple. Will the therapist schedule a few sessions with the mother and child together and see whether anything is amiss there? The assessment should also determine whether the girl has emotional problems or not. If there are problems, the mother certainly wants to begin therapy for her child and perhaps for herself as well. Also, information of this nature will be helpful to everyone involved and may clear up some issues in the custody dispute.

This sounds like a reasonable enough request, so the therapist agrees, adding that such an assessment may take several sessions, depending on the situation encountered. There is little time before the court hearing, so the mother and daughter are seen three times in the space of ten days. The therapist obtains a release from the mother, then reports to the attorney about the findings: The mother came across as caring and involved with the child; she evidenced a strong desire to have custody and felt that the father has not been a good influence; the girl does exhibit some problems, particularly in regard to her anger, which she often directs inward; her limp body tone and apathetic behavior suggest depression. She also exhibits self-hurting behavior such as punching herself in the arm after making a mistake. Some of these symptoms can be attributed to the parental separation, but further assessment and therapy are definitely indicated for the child.

The lawyer asks whether the therapist will write a report summarizing this information. Yes, certainly. This report is then filed with the court and a copy sent to the father's lawyer. Three days later the therapist receives an upset phone call from the father's lawyer, saying that it only seems fair for the father and daughter to be evaluated because the mother and daughter were evaluated. Can this be arranged? With some uneasiness, appointments are set up. It is all extremely rushed because the hearing date is now less than two weeks away. The girl looks much better in the presence of the father. She seems more lively, spontaneous, and playful. The father and daughter are observed to have exceptionally good rapport. The father appears to be genuinely concerned about the girl's welfare, speaks sensitively and appropriately about the child's needs, and relates many things about the mother's behavior toward the child that are of concern.

The father's attorney is pleased with this report and asks whether a written document can be prepared for court. With growing foreboding, this request is accommodated. Two days later, the therapist is handed a subpoena to appear in court to testify on behalf of the father.

The rest of the story can be told rather quickly, to spare us all of the unhappy details. On the witness stand, the therapist is asked by the father's lawyer whether the assessment indicated that there was a better relationship between father and daughter than between mother and daughter. It appeared so, yes, the therapist answers.

The attorney drives hard now, asking a series of intense questions that somehow lead to the therapist saying that the father should probably have custody of the child. On cross-examination, the mother's attorney turns into the enemy, endeavoring to discredit the therapist's credentials, procedures, and statements. The most damning of these challenges (because it is the most valid) is the question, "How could you presume to make a custody recommendation when no true evaluation had been carried out? Did you visit each of the parent's homes? Did you spend a sufficient amount of time with all parties? Did you contact this child's teacher and other significant professionals?" No, the witness concedes, these steps were not taken. Finally the therapist is dismissed from the stand, feeling angry, embarrassed, and confused.

The indignant mother never paid her bill. The father had paid for his few sessions in the office, but the two hours of court time were never compensated. In addition, the therapist had had to cancel a whole afternoon's appointments to be available in the court. All in all, it was a lousy experience and the therapist vowed never to become involved in a custody case again.

What Went Wrong?

Like a coach whose team has gone down in defeat, let us look at all the wrong moves made by the therapist in this situation. It began with that initial phone call from the attorney. To become involved in a custody dispute without clearly delineating one's role is always a mistake. The attorney, knowingly or unknowingly (probably the former), drew the mental health professional into the situation as a therapist but used him or her as an evaluator. Once the evaluator role was established, the opposing attorney began pulling the strings from the other side. In the end, no therapeutic purpose was served for the family. The involvement also failed as an evaluation.

Rule number one, then, is to keep the roles of therapist and evaluator separate. If a parent or an attorney approaches you to assess the emotional status of a child or parent, and the family is involved in custody litigation, ask whether this is for the purpose of therapy or evaluation. If for therapy, make it clear that you will not consent to testify if the matter should go to court. The parent or referring attorney should know that you will be firm about this. Some therapists even go as far as to ask parents to sign a short written contract saying that they will not ask the therapist to testify in a custody hearing. Lawyers differ in opinion as to whether this would really protect the professional from the courtroom. But it serves as a strong incentive for parents to keep their word. Perhaps its most important function is to sort out sincere from insincere intentions at the beginning of a case. If parents have a covert plan to drag in the therapist to serve their custody cause, presenting such a contract will discourage them and they will look elsewhere for a more complying witness.

When the mental health professional is asked to function as an evaluator, the nature of the case must be clarified right at the beginning. Most custody disputes fall into one of three categories. The first category is the most common. A marital separation has taken place and the parents disagree about who should have custody of the children. Legally, the parents have equal rights concerning the children until this is determined. A great deal of disruption sometimes characterizes these cases, with parents snatching the children back and forth from each other's households. To stabilize the situation, the court may order a temporary custody decree, dictating where the children will live until the case is resolved on a permanent basis.

The second type of evaluation requested is a "modification of custody." This occurs when custody has already been determined, but one party has asked the court to change it. For example, a couple divorced three years ago and the mother was given custody of their sons. The father now believes that the kids would do better in his care, and he has petitioned the court to make the change. An evaluation will help determine what will be in the children's best interests. In many states, however, "best interests" are not enough. The petitioner must demonstrate that it would harm the children to remain where they are. The evaluator must be aware of these factors in assessing the situation.

"Visitation evaluations" constitute the third type of service requested. Here, custody has already been determined, but difficulties have arisen over how much time the children should spend at each parent's household. Based on the ages, circumstances, and needs of the children, the evaluator recommends a beneficial time-sharing schedule.

Space limitations preclude the possibility of discussing modification and visitation evaluations in this manual. Undertaking such studies requires a specialized orientation that is gained only after considerable experience. Therefore, evaluators who are new to the field would be advised to postpone these involvements until later.

When a case is accepted, it is the evaluator, not the attorney, who sets the ground rules for its management. What are these ground rules? The following suggestions incorporate both ethical and practical considerations. Practitioners will want to adjust them to their individual circumstances. The term "litigants" is used to refer to the parties who are contesting custody, usually a mother and a father. It should be remembered, though, that in some instances litigants may be grandparents, aunts and uncles, or even biologically unrelated persons such as stepparents or friends of the family. Occasionally, four or more litigants have filed motions asking for custody of the same little child.

Groundrules for Doing
Custody Evaluations

(1) No evaluation will be undertaken unless attorneys for all litigants agree to it. Before the evaluator will set up appointments, he or she must have in hand a stipulation signed by the litigants agreeing to participate in the evaluation, or an order from the court requesting the evaluation.

(2) In every case, all litigants will be evaluated. The evaluator will refuse to evaluate just one party or to evaluate a child and litigant together without seeing the rest of the family. This rule applies even when one party is living out of state.

(3) The children in question will be observed in interaction with each litigant. Each child will be assessed individually and will be interviewed privately, if old enough.

(4) Visits will be made to the residence of each litigant at a time when all household members are present. The children in question must be at the residence at the time of the visit. If a litigant has traveled from out of state for the evaluation, provisions will be made to see that party with the children in a nonoffice setting.

(5) Each litigant will provide the evaluator with names of teachers, physicians, babysitters, and others who have been involved with the family. The parents will sign releases allowing the evaluator to talk to these collateral sources of information.

(6) The results of the evaluation will be written up in a report that will be sent to each attorney on the same day. If the evaluation was carried out under a court order, the evaluation will be filed in the appropriate court. No attorney or litigant will be told about the results of the evaluation in advance of others.

(7) Each litigant will be entitled to a feedback session with the evaluator after the reports are filed, providing an opportunity to ask questions, make comments, and obtain potentially helpful information concerning the children.

If the therapist in our story had established these guidelines before becoming involved in the case, there probably would have been no involvement at all. Few experienced evaluators would undertake an evaluation so close to the time of the final hearing. As a general rule, a custody study should not be started later than six weeks before the court date. They usually take at least a month to complete. Each step of the evaluation requires time. Scheduling appointments is sometimes difficult; key professionals whom the evaluator wants to contact are often hard to reach; pulling together results and writing the report should be done in an unhurried atmosphere. At least two weeks should be allowed after the report is filed to provide time for feedback sessions to take place, for attorneys to read the report and decide whether to call the evaluator to testify, and for the evaluator to prepare testimony. Furthermore, most states have laws requiring all documents to be filed with the court a certain number of days before the hearing. There are times when an evaluator may consent to do a "rush job" and frantically complete everything in a superhumanly short amount of time. He or she will live to regret it nine times out of ten.

Returning to the ground rules for evaluations, let us examine them in more detail.

Obtaining a stipulation or court order. A stipulation is an agreement. In this case, the contesting parties agree that the mental health professional will carry out a custody evaluation. Often the provisions for payment are delineated in the agreement. For example, "Mr. and Ms. Parent agree to share the cost of the evaluation equally and to pay their portions in full before the final report is released." A court order is a directive signed by the judge. In this instance it orders a custody evaluation to take place. It states which individual or agency shall perform the evaluation and names a date for completion. Other directives may be included in the order. An attorney can draw up the court order and ask the judge to sign it.

If you are working for a county or state agency that performs custody evaluations as part of its services, the stipulation or court order probably will already have been formalized by the time the case reaches you. If you are doing evaluations on a private practice basis, you will be responsible for making sure that you have a signed document in hand before proceeding. Mental health professionals could be more vulnerable to legal suit if they were to enter a person's home, assess their children, write a report that becomes a public record, and testify in court if they were not acting under a court order or stipulation. An irate parent could claim that he or she never really agreed to having a custody evaluation performed and that the therapist invaded privacy, betrayed confidences, and perpetrated all kinds of suit-worthy offenses.

Evaluating all contesting parties. The courts are familiar with those "hired gun" mental health professionals who, for a fee, will interview a parent and testify in court that this individual is certainly fit to have custody of the child. Seasoned judges have learned to recognize such testimony for what it is—courtroom game-playing that contributes little or nothing to the case. When therapists get a reputation for this kind of activity, their credibility in the legal and mental health community drops rapidly. This is not to say that they will not continue to be hired by certain lawyers, however.

A mental health professional is wise to establish a credible reputation from the beginning by maintaining high standards for custody evaluations. First and foremost is the insistence that all contesting parties be evaluated. The major difficulty in accomplishing this occurs when one parent is living out of state. In this case, the parent must either make arrangements to travel to the evaluator's location (which is where the court hearing will take place in most cases), or to send the evaluator to the parent's town. The latter option is usually extremely expensive. These arrangements have to be made well in advance and must be coordinated with the schedules of the evaluator, the other parent, and the children.

The children will be observed with each litigant and assessed individually. The quality of the parent-child relationship is one of the key factors in assessing where the children should live on a permanent basis. Observing the children with each parent, particularly in the home setting, is essential to a good custody evaluation. It is also important that each child's needs are assessed individually. Occasionally, siblings within the same family have different needs and preferences concerning their future living arrangements. Each child should be allowed ample time with the evaluator so that feelings, concerns, and information can be shared in a relaxed setting.

Visiting the homes of each litigant. If one parent lives out of town and is traveling in for the evaluation, arrangements should be made to see the parent and child together in a nonoffice setting. Because the parent probably once lived in the town where the hearing will take place, he or she will undoubtedly have a friend whose home can be borrowed for the occasion. In some cases, if hostilities are not too intense between the litigants, the visit can take place in the residential parent's house. For example, if the father is living with the children and the mother comes into town to participate in the evaluation, both home visits can take place in the same residence. During the mother-children visit, the father absents himself from the house for the afternoon. An advantage of this plan is that the children are already comfortable in their own familiar setting. A third option is for the visit to take place in the motel room, with a trip to a park or some other pleasant place. In all of these cases, information about the out-of-town parent's home environment will be gathered by long distance telephone interviews with friends and neighbors in the parent's present town.

Interviewing collaterals. Litigants should be aware from the beginning that you will be interviewing teachers, doctors, babysitters, acquaintances of the family, and other individuals in the course of the custody evaluation. During the first interview with the parents, each will be asked to sign releases for physicians, dentists, psychologists, and other professionals who have been involved with the family. As new information comes to light during the course of the custody study, the evaluator may find that other releases may need to be signed. For example, if the evaluator learns that one parent has been attending mandatory "alcohol education" class as part of an alcohol-related driving offense, the evaluator will need a release to talk to the counselor in charge.

Assembling a list of collaterals to call is facilitated by having each litigant fill out a personal data questionnaire in the beginning of the evaluation. On this questionnaire, parents are asked to list names of doctors, teachers, and others who have been involved with the family. They are also requested to write the names, addresses, and phone numbers of three persons who have knowledge of the family and who may be contacted to help shed light on the custody situation. A sample questionnaire appears as Figure 1.1.

Distributing the report and holding feedback sessions for litigants. To maintain the neutral stance emphasized throughout the evaluation, the results of the study should be shared with both con-

PERSONAL DATA SHEET

Name _____
        (last)   first)   (middle)

Address _____

Phone numbers (home)_____ (work) _____

Your attorney _ _____ (phone no.) _____

YOUR BACKGROUND

Birthdate _____ Age _____

Place of birth _____

Mother's name _____ If living, where does she reside? _____

Father's name _____ If living, where does he reside? _____

Number of sisters?_____ Brothers? _____

Your education: Highest year of school completed _____

List your marriages, starting with your first marriage:

Married to	Dates (from-to)	Names of Children	Children's birthdate	Children's address

Present employer _____ address _____

Your title or position _____ date employed _____

Work schedule _ _____ Gross salary_____ per_____

Please list last three positions and dates of employment:

Your living situation: House _____(renting _____ buying _____) Apt. _____

Monthly mortgage or rent _____

Number of persons sharing household _____

List persons in household_____

CHILDREN

Name	Birthdate	Address of primary residence	School or daycare	Grade

Children's doctor _____ phone number _____

Children's dentist _____ phone number _____

Children's therapist, if any _____ phone number _____

Please discuss any physical or emotional problems of your child(ren) which may have relevance for the custody situation.

In general, how have the children reacted to the separation?
Do you have any concerns about them now that should be discussed?

Figure 1.1 Sample Questionnaire

testing parties at the same time. This can be accomplished during brief sessions with each parent on the same day, or by distributing the report to both attorneys on the same day. One feels tempted occasionally to let a parent (or the lawyer) know what the recommendation of the report will be. But this information will instantly spread like wildfire, and the other side will feel justifiably resentful that they were not told in person. They will also wonder whether the evaluator had a special bond of some kind with the parties who were told the results in advance.

Why is it important to hold a feedback session with litigants? First, it contributes a more therapeutic tone to the whole process. To be evaluated for custody purposes is one of the most stressful experiences a parent can undergo. It can leave them feeling naked and defensive. A stranger has come into their lives, asking intimate questions, invading the privacy of their livingrooms, critiquing their lifestyles and parenting abilities, and making judgments about whether their children should live with them or not. When it is all over, they need to vent feelings and ask questions. To be merely handed a report and never have the opportunity to share their reactions with the evaluator would only add to the distress of their experience.

A second benefit of the feedback session is educational in nature. Often the evaluator has detailed information to share about the children that could not be included in the report because of length limitations. The evaluator may have seen patterns operating within the family that could only be explained adequately face-to-face, not in a court report. Perhaps the evaluator wishes to encourage a parent to go into therapy to deal with the emotions that they have been experiencing. This can be accomplished most effectively in person. For some families, this will be their first and last opportunity to be viewed by a mental health professional. The feedback session maximizes this contact.

Stylistically, evaluators differ on how to organize this final session. Many of them distribute the report and then schedule appointments with each litigant after everyone has had time to receive and read the report. Some evaluators see the parents together;

some hold separate sessions. An alternative method is to hold the feedback session before the report is actually distributed. The parents are asked to come to the office together and are told the results of the evaluation in person. They are each given a copy of the report and asked to read it carefully. Then they are each encouraged to voice their feelings and reactions. This method has distinct merits. Parents may witness in person the feelings and reactions of each other and even begin to talk openly together. I have heard many parents say, "If you recommend against me in this evaluation, my husband (or wife) will laugh with glee." This is a fiction that arises out of the pain of custody conflict. In truth, few parents ever laugh with glee at finding out they have been recommended for custody. Most commonly, they report feeling "relieved, but sad, too, because I know how terrible my ex-spouse must feel." Being together in the room can bring reality to this crucial moment. Some evaluators use this intense session to discuss visitation (which is best called "time-sharing"), seeing if there are grounds for a meeting of the minds on this important subject.

The evaluator may also benefit by holding a feedback session before the report is finalized. Small inaccuracies in the report can be corrected. A parent may say, "No, we didn't move to Milwaukee in 1980, that was 1979. And our son never lived with his father's aunt; it was my aunt." The evaluator can make minor changes in the report before it is distributed to the court or to attorneys.

Some evaluators take the feedback session a step further and use it to attempt to mediate the dispute. They reason that perhaps they can assist the parents in resolving their differences and agree to a custody and visitation arrangement. I disagree with this approach. Mediation is the most hopeful trend in child custody today and should be encouraged in every case. But interjecting it into the middle of an evaluation is a matter of wrong timing. The appropriate times to attempt mediation are before the evaluation begins or after the evaluation is completed. This mediation should be undertaken by someone other than the evaluator. Blurring the two roles is confusing to all parties, creates interpersonal entanglements for the mental health professional, and could have complicated legal ramifications. For example, in many states, information shared in the context of mediation does not necessarily have to be revealed on the witness stand, but information gathered in the course of an evaluation generally must be disclosed. If a couple wants to mediate after the custody study is over, the evaluator should refer them to someone else for this service.

Fees

Our sympathy goes out to the therapist in the account who not only lost face and faith, but fees as well. By following a few basic rules, this never would have happened:

(1) Establish a general fee range before agreeing to the evaluation. Generally, therapists charge a per-hour fee that is equivalent to their therapy per-hour fee. They estimate the number of hours an evaluation will take and multiply this by their hourly rate. The attorneys are then told that the evaluation will cost around a certain amount, give or take a few hours. Estimating how many hours to allot to an evaluation is difficult without experience. Many factors will determine the length of a study. How many parties are involved? If custody of only one child is being contested, the number of hours required to complete the evaluation will be shorter than if custody of three children is being contested. If each parent is remarried and stepchildren are involved, this will add time. Are there allegations of battering, child abuse, or drug involvement? These are red flags to the evaluator that the case will be additionally time consuming. There is no standard formula for estimating the length of an evaluation, but sixteen hours can be considered a minimum amount of time for a study involving two parents and one child. For each additional child or stepparent to be interviewed two hours could be added. These estimates do not include "mulling it

over" time, but rather represent direct involvement hours. The breakdown on an 18-hour evaluation (two parents, two children) may look like this:

office interviews:	4 hours
home visits:	6 hours (add for travel if relevant)
collateral interviews:	2 ½ hours
report preparation:	3 hours
feedback sessions:	1 ½ hours (45 minutes for each parent)
Total:	18 hours

(2) Once the fee is established, the evaluator should request that a retainer of one half of the total be paid before the first interviews are held. The other half is payable in full before the results are shared with anyone. This rule accomplishes two goals. It reinforces the notion that the evaluator is an independent agent who will be getting paid no matter what the report says. If, say, the father still owed his fee and the evaluator recommended for the father, the other side could say, "Of course the recommendation favored him; that evaluator knew that he or she would never see a penny unless the father was favored." Second, requiring payment in advance assures that the evaluator will be compensated. Otherwise, valuable time and energy will have to be spent trying to collect from an angry parent after the report is released.

(3) The fee does not include testimony time if the evaluator should have to go to court. If subpoenaed, the evaluator will ask for a retainer covering a half day's clinical fees. It is rare that an evaluator will know exactly when he or she will be called to the witness stand during the hearing. Much time will be spent waiting, and this must be compensated. If it turns out that testimony is short and client hours can be salvaged, an equivalent portion of the retainer will be returned.

Mental health professionals are notorious for feeling shy about money. But having a firm policy about the financial arrangements of a custody evaluation will elicit increased respect from attorneys, who tend not to be shy about requiring compensation for their services. Most important, it will save one the unenviable fate of having to fight monetary battles long after the custody battles are over.

CONTINUING CASE STUDY
Norcross vs. Norcross

At the end of each chapter, data from a custody evaluation will be presented in the form of an evaluator's notes. The type of information included will correspond to the subject matter of the chapter. Therefore, this section covers preliminary arrangements for undertaking the evaluation. The "Norcross" case is a composite of several families. It embodies custody issues that are often encountered. In order to develop the situation properly, these narratives will display more detail than would an evaluator's actual case notes.

Last Monday I received a call from an attorney named Alfred Chappell. He told me that he represented the mother in a custody case and would like to retain me as as an evaluator. The family's name is Norcross. This situation is fairly clearcut, he indicated, and would probably not go to court. The couple separated in January shortly after the holidays. Things were somewhat amicable between them until the mother filed for divorce a month later. The father filed a counter motion asking for custody of their four-and-a-half-year-old son. As happens so often, the father is using this as a ploy to draw the mother back into the marriage. But his attorney won't back down, and insists on an evaluation.

Given the situation, what the family needs is the least complicated, most economical evaluation possible. "What we really want is a mini-evaluation," he said. He suggested that perhaps I could see the child once, have an interview with each parent, and leave it at that.

I told him that I understood what he was saying but that I could not accommodate his request. All of my evaluations were thorough, indepth studies involving multiple interviews, home visits, and contact with parties outside the family. I would not become involved in a case under any other circumstances. He sounded disappointed at this. I offered to send him a brief description of my evaluation procedures, so that he could share this with his client. Mr. Chappell asked for an estimate of the cost of doing the kind of evaluation I described. How many family members were involved, I inquired? A mother, a father, the child in question, and an eight-year-old girl by the mother's previous marriage. Were there any allegations of abuse, alcoholism, drug involvement, arrests, or similar problems? Not to his knowledge. Based on this information, the evaluation would require around 18 hours of clinical time. I quoted him an estimated fee. But if complications arose, the fee could run somewhat higher. This estimate did not include testimony time, of course, if the case went to court.

I sent the evaluation description, not expecting to hear from Mr. Chappell again. It would be easy for him to find someone who would take a cursory look at the family and write a brief report.

A week later I received a call from Susan Gomez, attorney for the father in the Norcross case. She had spoken to Mr. Chappell about the evaluation. She liked the completeness of my procedures and was considering going ahead with the evaluation. She thought Mr. Chappell might agree to it also because she was taking a strong stand on having a full evaluation. In fact, she felt confident that she could get a court order requiring such an evaluation. But Ms. Gomez had some questions to ask me first. She was concerned about my views toward fathers having custody. Many professionals still favored mothers. This issue was particularly important in the present case because the child was so young. She referred to the "tender years presumption" that guided many courts and evaluators in the recent past. It maintained that children in the early, "tender years" needed to be with their mothers.

It was important that we discuss this, I responded. An evaluator should always be clear about his or her orientation. I said that my work was focused on one question only: "What living situation will be best for this child, now and in the future?" I viewed mothers and fathers as equally capable of rearing children. Infants and young children could establish deep emotional bonds to fathers as well as to mothers. The determining factors did not center around the sex of the parent, but around issues such as the needs and attachments of the child, the total physical, emotional, and intellectual environment that each parent offered, and the quality of the child-parent relationship. I also strongly supported the continued involvement of both parents in the child's life, no matter who had custody.

Just how many fathers had I actually recommended for in my evaluations, Ms. Gomez asked? "This is one tough attorney," I found myself thinking. But I did not feel that it was appropriate for me to share that information with her. So I said, "I have a good record for recommending custody to fathers as well as mothers. But this is not a numbers game. I'll be evaluating which parent best meets the needs of this particular little boy." That appeared to satisfy her. If not, at least she did not press the point.

Ms. Gomez then began telling me about the case, implying what a marvelous father Mr. Norcross was. I broke in gently with, "Ms. Gomez, I think it would be better to discuss this later. We have not finalized arrangements for an evaluation yet. And if we do proceed, I'd like to start out on neutral ground with both parents." I added that if the parents signed a stipulation, I would appreciate being sent copies of all pleadings concerning the custody issue. This would give me valuable background on the case.

Apparently seeing no point in continuing our conversation, she thanked me and left me with a brisk goodbye.

2

Preparing for the
Final Report

Doesn't the final report belong to the last stage of the process rather than to the first? No. All phases of a custody evaluation should be carried out with the report in mind. Knowing what is required in the written document helps structure our information gathering. It cues us as to what should be emphasized in our notes and which lines of questioning will be useful.

Report writers get bogged down trying to say too much. How often have we seen long, tedious documents that have no clear line of development? The writer has tried to cram in every scrap of information, and the thoughts circle around and around like buzzards uncertain of where to light. Then, in a brief "recommendation" paragraph, the evaluator suddenly blurts out the decision. Attorneys and judges invariably say, "I have read all 18 pages of this, and I still don't see how the evaluator arrived at this recommendation." That report has failed in its task.

Generally, the report's line of development will parallel that of the evaluation itself. We will want to establish a history of the case, review each parent's allegations, concerns, and feelings about having custody, and summarize important information that arises. "Important" information will usually center around the questions,

"What are the needs and feelings of this child? How does each parent appear to meet these needs—physically, emotionally, and socially? How well can each parent be expected to meet these needs in the future?" Finally, we will apply our reasoning and explain why the facts point to recommending custody for litigant "A" rather than litigant "B." The report is not complete at this point. Specific time-sharing recommendations should be made so that the child will gain maximum benefit from continued contact with both parents.

Stylistic details of report writing will be treated later. For now, it is enough to convey the general structure of a good custody report. The following example can serve as a model. It does not represent the only approach possible, nor does it pretend to be the best evaluation ever written. But it is clear, orderly, behaviorally oriented, and makes its point. Naturally, the names and circumstances have been fictionalized.

CUSTODY EVALUATION REPORT
Re: Marks vs. Marks
Court Case No. 12-3456-7

Children in Question

Melissa Marks, almost seven years old
Phillip Marks, three years old

Evaluator

Dianne Skafte, M.A.

Participants in this Evaluation

Janice Marks, mother (d.o.b. 7/6/55)
Ronald Marks, father (d.o.b. 10/2/46)
Melissa Marks, daughter (d.o.b. 9/13/78)
Phillip Marks, son (d.o.b. 3/17/82)

Procedures

At the stipulation of both parties, a custody evaluation was carried out concerning Melissa and Phillip Marks. The mother and father were interviewed in separate office sessions. Home visits were made to the residence of each parent at a time when both children were present. Melissa and Phillip were observed in interaction with family members and were interviewed privately during each of these visits. In addition, telephone interviews were held with the following persons:

Dr. Frederick Tallis, the children's physician
Mr. John Hoem, Melissa's second-grade teacher at
    Valley Elementary School
Ms. Martha Egan, Jason's daycare teacher at Valley
    Elementary School
Ms. Wanda Jenkins, the children's babysitter
Mr. Fred Black, the father's employer at the Flatirons Airport
Ms. Doris Daner, the mother's supervisor, County Tax
    Assessor's Office
Ms. Marcy Blooms, reference provided by the father
Ms. Cynthia Walker, reference provided by the father
Mr. Hal Huntley, reference provided by the mother
Ms. Patricia Taylor, reference provided by the mother

Background and Allegations

Mr. and Mrs. Marks were married in 1975 after having known each other for almost a year. The couple reported that their relationship went well for about three years but began to deteriorate after the birth of their first child. A series of increasingly bitter disputes about money, jealousy, and child-rearing issues led to several temporary marital separations. The final separation occurred in June of this year, when the mother left the household with the children and rented an apartment a mile away. The father remained in the family residence. In July, the father picked up the children from school and took them to his house, maintaining that they should be living with him. He declined to return them to the mother when she requested him to do so. Two weeks later the children were returned to their mother's residence under a temporary custody order. They have lived with Ms. Marks to the present, seeing their father on alternate weekends from 5:00

Friday until 5:00 Sunday, and on each Wednesday from 5:00 to 7:00 p.m.

It is Mr. Mark's position that he could offer the children a better environment than could Ms. Marks. He alleged that Ms. Marks "coddles the children too much," cannot handle money, and does not maintain high moral standards. Mr. Marks said that he would provide the right kind of guidance to build the children's character, including religious training. This would not be available in the mother's home, he stressed. The father also expressed concern that Ms. Marks has a boyfriend who spends the night, creating an undesirable and immoral influence on the children.

Ms. Marks reported that she fears for the children's welfare if the father were to receive custody. She described him as "overly authoritarian" and said that the children are frightened of him. Ms. Marks maintained that she has carried most of the responsibility for the children's care over the years and that the father has not been actively involved in everyday aspects of their lives. The mother believes that Melissa and Phillip would be unhappy living away from her.

Evaluation of Family Members

JANICE MARKS (MOTHER)

Ms. Marks reported having a warm family relationship with her own parents during her childhood and adolescence. She still visits her parents in Illinois about twice a year. The major problems growing up as she described them were "shyness" and "insecurity." She married Mr. Marks, nine years her senior, because she was attracted to his competency and "strong character." Ms. Marks reported that after the birth of Melissa, Mr. Marks seemed to become more "dictatorial" and demanding, appearing to resent the attention she paid to the baby and accusing her of flirting with other men. No physical violence took place in the household. Ms. Marks decided to leave the marriage several times but was persuaded to return, she said. In June she separated permanently.

Ms. Marks has been employed with the County Tax Assessor's office for two years as a clerk. She intends to keep that job for several more years. Ms. Marks acknowledged that she has been seeing a man named John, whom she referred to as "a good friend and nothing more." He comes over to the house for dinner and to watch television sometimes, but has never spent the night, she reports. She does not believe that the children have been hurt in any way by this relationship.

Ms. Marks's plan, if she received custody of the children, would be to move back into the family home if possible, or rent a townhouse if the house were sold. She would leave Melissa and Jason in their present schools because she feels that the children are doing well there. During the summer Melissa would go to Phillip's daycare school, which offers a summer program.

During the office interview, Ms. Marks appeared to be timid and unsure of herself. She had to be encouraged to express her opinions and to relate concerns about the custody situation. In her home environment, she was markedly more relaxed. She dealt with the children warmly and attentively, setting up activities for them to do and directing their behavior effectively without having to coerce them. It was noted, however, that she succumbed to Phillip's repeated request to bring the dog into the house, despite her previous refusals of that request.

Collateral interviewees who were contacted tended to view Ms. Marks as an "excellent mother" who "does a lot" for her children. Interviewees described many activities that Ms. Marks participates in with other parents and children. Melissa's teacher and Phillip's daycare teacher reported that Ms. Marks maintains frequent contact with them and attends school activities regularly. The daycare teacher reported that it is generally Ms. Marks rather than Mr. Marks who has delivered and picked up Phillip from daycare for the last year.

RONALD MARKS (FATHER)

Mr. Marks described his upbringing as "strict but loving" in a "good religious home" in Missouri. He has good memories of childhood until he was fourteen years old when his mother was killed in a car-train accident while out with a friend at night. A year later, his father remarried a woman who was only five years older than Mr. Marks. This created some problems in the household, but they were never discussed, according to Mr. Marks. This marriage ended in divorce a few years later. At age eighteen, Mr. Marks joined the Airforce and learned airplane maintenance, an occupation he still pursues today. Mr. Marks reported that he has not seen his father for about eight years, but that he plans to visit next summer.

In the private interview, Mr. Marks focused a great deal on the marital separation, expressing his desire to have the family reunited again. He said that he maintained the hope that the mother would "come to her senses." Mr. Marks appeared to be most comfortable when discussing general principles and guidelines for rearing children. He clearly has given a great deal of thought to these issues and is concerned that his children receive the right guidance. He was less at ease in discussing Melissa's and Phillip's feelings, development, and everyday needs. He was unaware, for example, of who Melissa's friends are or what her favorite subjects are in school.

If he were to have custody of the children, Mr. Marks would like to remain in the family home with them. He was somewhat vague about his plans for caring for Melissa and Phillip, saying that he might "hire a woman" to come in after school. He did stress that he would make sure the children attended church with him each Sunday morning.

During the home visit, Mr. Marks directed the children's behavior very specifically, telling them, for example, when to interact with the evaluator and when to go to their rooms to play. It was noted that the children complied easily with his directives. For example, when Phillip asked to go out bike riding rather than interact with the evaluator, Mr. Marks denied the request and the child did not bring it up again. Positive interaction was observed between Mr. Marks and Phillip when the boy asked questions about the space shuttle. The father devoted time and patience to explaining things carefully in a way that was easily understandable.

Collateral interviewees described Mr. Marks as "a good man," "a reliable person," and "a person of conviction." None of the informants had seen him alone with the children and so could not comment on his behavior as a father. Mr. Marks was praised highly by his employer at the Flatirons Airport for his excellent performance during the last five years.

MELISSA MARKS (DAUGHTER)

Melissa came across as a quiet, observant girl who endeavored to please the adults around her. With the evaluator, she enjoyed the activity of making up fantasy stories. Recurring themes involved a girl heroine who tries hard to please a male authority figure but does not succeed. For example, in one story, a girl puppet dances for a king but falls through a trap door when he pushes a button. Melissa expressed anxiety around the custody situation, fearing that one of her parents would end up angry. She was assured that she would not have to choose between her parents. In discussing the "best things" and "worst things" about being at each parent's home, Melissa was able to relate in detail things she liked about being with her mother. She had difficulty in relating feelings, positive or negative, about being with her father. On being encouraged to respond, she conveyed that she enjoys going to church with him and misses doing so on the weekends she is away.

During the home visits, Melissa's behavior was observed to be markedly different in the presence of each parent. She played and laughed spontaneously at her mother's residence, interacting occasionally with Phillip, but often creating her own activities. At her father's house, she appeared to be cautious and controlled, watching him for cues on what to do. She hovered around her brother and took a mothering role towards him, getting him drinks and trying to attend to his needs.

PHILLIP MARKS (SON)

Phillip, who will be four years old next month, is well developed physically and intellectually. He carried on conversations with ease and was able to write a few letters of the alphabet. His mother taught him to do this, he said. Phillip's teacher reported that the boy gets along well with other children in the daycare center but tends to boss them around at times. She attributes this to his superior verbal abilities.

In fantasy games with stuffed animals initiated by the evaluator, Phillip placed the baby bear in a cave with the "momma bear" rather than with the "daddy bear." He also objected when the evaluator had a "boy puppy" go away on a trip with the daddy dog. When asked why, he said, "He'll miss his mommy, stupid!"

During the home visits, Phillip showed a great deal of affection to each parent, climbing into their laps and asking them many questions. He tended to be more demanding with his mother, testing the limits often with her. With his father he was more cooperative. At the father's home, Phillip also tended to depend on Melissa a great deal for assistance. This behavior was not observed at his mothers' house.

Conclusions

Interviews with both parents as well as with collaterals suggest that the mother has been the primary caretaker of these children from the time they were infants. She has demonstrated an ability to understand the needs of the children and to attend to them appropriately. Although Mr. Marks clearly loves Melissa and Phillip, he appears to be out of touch with the practical and emotional realities of what little children need and feel. The family atmosphere at the mother's home offers the children a warmer and more open context for developing than does that of the father.

Communications from both children indicate that they do not want to live away from their mother. This evaluator also has concern that Melissa would too readily take on a caretaking role with Phillip at her father's home and thereby become increasingly burdened and serious.

These factors point to a recommendation that the children live with their mother. However, the father's importance in the children's lives is crucial. Melissa's desire to win his approval and Phillip's obvious enjoyment of his presence are further evidence of this. Mr. Marks's involvement in their religious educations appears to be an especially positive factor in their relationship with him. A time-sharing plan should therefore support this involvement.

Melissa and Phillip would benefit by spending a little time alone with each parent during the year. A summer time-sharing schedule that affords this is recommended.

It is further suggested that both Mr. and Ms. Marks enter into family counseling with the children or participate in parenting skills classes. Mr. Marks could improve his relationship with the children by learning to understand their feelings and needs more sensitively. Ms. Marks could benefit by learning to deal more effectively with Phillip's assertiveness, which will increase as he becomes older. Ms. Marks could also work on self-esteem issues.

Recommendations

(1) That the mother have custody of Melissa and Phillip.

(2) That the father have the children each weekend from Saturday 5:00 p.m. to Sunday 7:00 p.m., and each Wednesday after school (or at 3:00 p.m. in the summer) until 7:00 p.m. In two years, when Phillip is six and Melissa is nine, an alternate weekend schedule may work better for the children. It is suggested that the family enlist the assistance of a counselor mediator to adjust the schedule at this time.

(3) That holidays be alternated each year between the parents, beginning with the father having Christmas with the children this year.

(4) Summer vacation for Philip: Because of his dependency on his mother at this time, it is recommended that Phillip spend three separate one-week periods of summer vacation with his father during the upcoming summer. This should increase to two separate two-week periods for the following two summers. Thereafter, he should spend half of each summer with the father.

(5) Summer vacation for Melissa: Two separate two-week periods for the next three summers, overlapping with

Phillip's time, if desired. Thereafter, half of each summer should be spent with her father.
(6) That both parents participate in family therapy or parenting skills classes.

Several points are worth mentioning about the format of this report because they give us clues on effective information gathering. Notice that the history was kept short and focused on major facts only, particularly those concerning the children's living arrangement. History-taking during interviews can be economized if it follows the same guidelines. Parents are generally eager to discuss all the details of their marriage and separation. It is easy to spend an hour and a half with a parent and hear what appears to be meaningful material about everyone's actions, upsets, and intrigues. It is only later (perhaps while writing the report) that you realize you know nothing about where the children lived during all of these comings and goings. Parents themselves do not tend to emphasize this type of information. Yet the report must clearly outline how long the couple was married, when they separated, and who had possession of the children during various periods.

The paragraphs describing the allegations of each parent are more difficult to write than one might think. Some litigants walk into the initial interview with their allegations all ready to present in clear form. The evaluator then takes careful notes and summarizes them in the report. More often, however, parents present vague or tangled material that must be sorted through. For example, the evaluator asks a father what concerns he has about the mother's parenting. The conversation proceeds as follows:

Father: She's a good mother but she doesn't think, you know? She doesn't use her head. I know she loves the children.

Evaluator: Can you give me an example of when you felt she didn't use her head?

Father: Well, there are lots of examples. She had Ronald in one of those frame carriers that you put on your back. She took it off, with him still in it, and set it up on the couch. Then she walked away. The baby threw himself sideways and fell right over the side, pack and all, and landed on his head. I can name dozens of things. Last week, Johnny, our six-year-old, told me he woke up in the middle of the night and couldn't find his mother. He was scared and began crying. His mother had driven to the 7-11 store. Now that's almost a 20-minute drive down the mountain just one way. Who knows how long she was gone?

Evaluator: So you feel that the children's mother doesn't use good judgment in caring for the children at times.

Father: Exactly. I'd say that she uses damn poor judgment.

Evaluator: Is there anything else that concerns you about her parenting?

In this way, the parent is helped to organize the myriad of thoughts and experiences that are often difficult for them to put into words. In the above example, the final report would summarize the father's position as follows: "The father maintains that the mother frequently uses poor judgment in caring for the children. He related numerous examples of behavior that he feels has endangered Ronald and Johnny." The report will probably not relate the specifics of these. This would require too much space and is unnecessary. The father's attorney already knows the details, and if the matter goes to court, the father himself can give this testimony to the judge.

Helping parents to express their concerns as specifically as possible during the interviews is important for two reasons. First and foremost, it will alert us to problem areas in the family and will help direct the course of inquiry. In the example just related, the evaluator will now pay close attention to the mother's judgment about the children. This will be accomplished by watching her with the children and discussing matters of judgment with her (i.e., "How would you handle the situation if your son cut himself badly with a knife?"). Reports from teachers and others who have seen her with the children would also provide information.

Second, if we fail to arrive at a clear understanding of key allegations and concerns, the parent and/or the attorney will certainly come back after reading the report and say, "You never even heard my (or my client's) point of view." It won't matter that we tried several times unsuccessfully to get the parent to express him- or herself.

Occasionally a litigant persistently cannot offer any information on this issue. It is then advisable to ask the person to go home and write a list of concerns, having the attorney help him or her if necessary. In this way we obtain a written account if the matter should come up later. I did this with a mother who continually became vague and changed the subject when I tried to interview her on this matter. Although I asked her to have her attorney help her make the suggested list, she did not do so. The paper that she gave me in the next session simply said, "He's a good father. I can't think of anything that's not good. I guess he plays with them too much sometimes." It became clear later in the evaluation that she did not really feel that the children should live with her but was responding to pressure from her parents to obtain custody. At the end of the evaluation, she expressed open relief when I recommended the father as custodial parent.

The sections evaluating each family member contain information that must be gathered in the evaluation. The first paragraph on each parent summarized a little of his or her personal background. Of special importance are those factors that might influence parenting. Litigants' relationships with their own parents, past and present, is important information. In the Marks's case, the mother clearly had a better connection with her own family than did the father, who had not seen his parents for eight years. Because the extended family was not a crucial issue for these particular children (sometimes it is), the report did not emphasize this difference in the "conclusion" section. But the facts were duly noted in the report. When interviewing parents in a custody evaluation, little time is available to dwell on childhood and background issues. Questions must be posed that will emphasize the information desired. Suggestions for doing this are included in Chapter 3.

The sample report also contained paragraphs describing each litigant's plans for taking care of the children in the future. This question is important enough to ask more than once. Approaching it in the initial session and again during the home visit seems to work well. A parent who cannot focus in on this issue probably has not given it much thought. This fact should be noted by the evaluator. A surprising number of litigants ask for custody, not because they truly want primary responsibility for the children, but because of hidden motives. Perhaps they hope for a reunification of the family and secretly feel that the partner will come back in order to be with the children. (We suspected this to be true in the Marks's case.) Perhaps the parent does not want to "lose face" by losing custody of the children. This common sentiment results from the structure of the court system that emphasizes "winning" and "losing." Possibly the parent feels too guilty to give the other spouse custody voluntarily.

Careful notes should be taken on all statements that parents make about their children. We need to understand how well litigants understand their children's needs and feelings, and how accurate their perceptions are concerning them. When asked how he felt his son was doing in school, one father commented that the boy was "smart but lazy." Later, the father was asked whether he felt his son had any particular problems that were of concern. The father said again that laziness was the boy's only problem. An interview with the school psychologist revealed that the child had a learning disability and had been in special education classes for three years. What does this indicate about the father's insight into his own child?

Other material selected for the sample report included observations of the parent-child relationship, data about the child's feelings and behavior, and pertinent information from the home visit. Information gathered from collateral interviewees (those not connected with the case) was used sparingly, and only to support key issues and concerns. Some of the worst reports I have ever seen earned that rating because they included too much useless information about what collaterals said to them. This paragraph is typical:

Ms. Higgins related to this evaluator that the mother and father fought often during the marriage. She said she was sure that they were drinking because the mother had told her that they both drank a lot. Ms. Higgins also related that one night in February of this year, the father threw the mother into a snowbank at 2:00 a.m. This was after the mother had thrown the father's car keys up into a tree.

The conclusions section should be kept as tight and efficient as possible. This is not the place for a lot of psychological subtleties or general gabbing about the case. All too often while presenting his or her conclusions, the writer suddenly gets inspired to give a speech about something or other. This is distracting for judges and attorneys.

From the opening hours of the custody study, the evaluator is preparing to write the conclusions and recommendations. The data are continually being scanned for emerging patterns. What pieces of information fit with each other? Which pieces contradict each other? What is missing and needs to be filled in? What are the key issues developing in this case? For example, in the case of Marks, the evaluator noticed immediately that the father had difficulty concentrating on the issue of the children. Did this result from a lack of involvement with them? Or was he just not good at expressing himself? Later it was seen that he dealt with the children in a rather rigid, rule-oriented manner that lacked emotional warmth. But this parenting style is not necessarily bad for children. What did the mother's parenting style have to offer? Did the children need her easy, open, sometimes too weak approach more than they needed their father's too firm hand? Further investigation revealed that the children saw their mother as their major source of security, and they expressed the desire to be with her most of the time. Interviews with collaterals confirmed that, indeed, the mother had been much more closely involved with the children over the years than the father. The pattern was clearer now. The mother could provide a better home base for the children. The children could benefit from the father's love and guidance by having frequent contact with him. The time-sharing plan supported the father's desire to provide religious education to the children. These adult needs should always be considered, as long as they do not interfere with the children's best interests. If a plan is to work, it must offer something of value to each family member.

Preparing for the final report really means maintaining a clear notion of where one is heading. No evaluation can eliminate the thorns from the thicket of divorce. But it can recommend the safest and least entangled routes to the children's future well being.

CONTINUING CASE STUDY
Norcross vs. Norcross

Surprisingly, a letter arrived from Mr. Chappell with a signed stipulation, a check from his client, and a note saying that they were pleased to have this evaluation. A few days later I received Ms. Gomez's client's check and the legal papers that I had requested.

I scanned the documents. Generally they spell out allegations against the other parent and state reasons why the petitioner is asking for custody. Reading these pleadings is useful for selecting the questions I will ask each parent in the first interview.

The mother's petition asks that she be awarded custody of Angelo (the four-year-old) on several grounds. It maintains that the child wished to live with her and has stated this desire on numerous occasions. It asserts that the mother will be more attentive to Angelo's educational needs because she herself is better educated than the father and is more attuned to these issues. It alleges that the father is unable to provide Angelo with adequate everyday care and is particularly negligent about his nutrition. It further states that Angelo should not be separated from his stepsister, with whom he has lived most of his life.

The father's petition is shorter. It states simply that he can offer the child a more stable, affectionate home than the mother can, and that he requests a custody evaluation to help determine the best interests of Angelo. The brevity of this approach struck me as somewhat unusual. Did the father really have little grounds for his plea, as Mr. Chappell suggested? Or did this reflect Ms. Gomez's style of drafting petitions? We would see.

I made notes to include the following areas in my interviews with the parents: (1) On what does the mother base her belief that Angelo wants to live with her? Have there been other indications other than his statements? In listening to her, I planned to note how sensitive she appeared to be to his feelings; I would also try to discern whether she had put any kind of pressure on him concerning the custody issue. (2) The mother is more educated than the father? What does that mean? What are her concerns about Angelo's education? (3) What leads the mother to say that the father is unable to provide adequate everyday care? I need details here. (4) In what specific ways does the father believe he can offer Angelo a more stable and affectionate home? Why does he believe that the mother's environment does not measure up to his in this respect? What other strengths does he believe he has as a parent? In addition to these specific questions, I will want to get a good history of the marriage and separation. What has been the pattern of time sharing with both children since the separation? How does the stepsister, Lisa, fit into all of this?

I called Ms. Norcross and introduced myself. I expected her to sound a bit apprehensive in this initial contact, as most parents do. But she seemed warm and at ease.

"I would like to see you and Mr. Norcross together for the first session," I said. "I hope this won't be a problem for either of you."

"It won't be a problem for me," she answered. "My emotional separation from this marriage is just about complete. I don't know how much of the history you are acquainted with, but I am the one who left the relationship. I have a feeling that Jacob may object to a joint interview, though. I'm afraid he hasn't adjusted very well to the reality of the divorce."

"I see. I'll want to explore this further during the interview," I said, not wanting to pursue it on the telephone. "Right now I would like us to select two possible times for an interview. Then I will call Mr. Norcross and see whether one of them will suit his schedule."

Having established these appointment times, I called the father. "This is Jacob Norcross," the youngish voice said. "I'm sure sorry that you have to talk to this darned machine. But if you would leave your name and number . . ."

The next morning, he returned my call. He sounded a little breathless and anxious and had to ask me several times to repeat myself. I asked him whether he was acquainted with the steps of the custody evaluation. He hesitated. I offered to review them, and he said that he would appreciate that.

"I'll be spending about an hour and a half with you and Ms. Norcross together," I said, "to obtain a history of the marriage and to ask both of you questions about Angelo and Lisa. This will be a time for you express ideas and concerns you may have about custody, about the children's futures, and other matters. Next I will see you alone in my office for about an hour so that we can cover other issues. I'll make arrangements with you to come out to your house sometime during the next few weeks. Angelo needs to be there, because I want to spend time alone with him. In the meantime, I'd like you to be thinking of people I might talk to by telephone who could provide additional information. After the study is completed, I will ask you to come into the office once more and I will discuss the results with you. Did you have any questions?"

"Are you sure you want to see us together?" he asked.

"Yes. It will help the evaluation. Is that a problem for you?"

"Jenny is a problem for me, everything about her. I feel bad seeing her, that's all."

"I think I can understand that. The session will last only an hour and a half. I will do my best to keep things under control so that the conversation stays constructive," I said.

"I'll come, all right, don't worry about that. I just . . . well, never mind."

"I appreciate your cooperation; thank you. Let's look at these two dates and times and see if either of them works for you."

We agreed on the time of the meeting and said goodbye. Mr. Norcross said the word reluctantly, as though he had much more to say. Of course he did. I only hoped that he would be able to say it, at least part of it, in the presence of Ms. Norcross.

3

Interviewing
Litigants

Two formats are available for interviewing parents in the initial session. In the first, the mother and father are asked to come to the office together. In the second, separate appointments are made with each parent. These arrangements require slightly different interviewing approaches.

Having the parents come to the office together produces more emotional stress for everyone involved, but also yields more valuable information. Parents will often object to this arrangement, saying that they positively will not sit in the room with that (expletive deleted). The evaluator can answer along the lines of, "I know it is not a pleasant prospect for you, but I'm afraid it is necessary for this evaluation. I will stop the session if it looks as though things are getting too intense for anyone." If objections are still raised, the counselor should ask the parent exactly what he or she fears might happen in a joint session. Often parents have trouble putting their concerns into words. The evaluator should spend a few minutes helping them express themselves. Some of the fears commonly expressed are: "I'm afraid I'll break down and cry"; "I'm afraid I will lose my temper completely and the whole thing will turn into a shouting match"; "He (or she) will run right over me again, like always, and I'll just clam up and won't be able to say anything."

The evaluator should assure them that every effort will be made to keep the session constructive for all parties. Interpersonal abusiveness will certainly not be tolerated. With these assurances, most litigants are able to consent to a joint interview.

If one of the parties has reason to believe that violence may take place between the couple, the evaluator should exercise caution in encouraging a joint meeting. A few questins will help determine whether the fears are grounded or not. Has there ever been physical abuse or violence in the family before? Has the partner threatened to harm anyone in the recent past? Do either of the parties lose their tempers easily, tend to throw things, or strike out physically? If the answer to any of these questions is yes, a joint session should not be risked.

Once the couple is in the room, it helps to acknowledge that this is not an easy situation for them; (e.g., "I suspect that it is not easy for you two to be in a joint session together. But this whole evaluation is taking place for the sake of the children, and I appreciate your consenting to be here.") It is usually better not to try to make "small talk" in an attempt to put them at ease. It won't work because their emotions are too intense.

An effective way to begin the interview is to address the neutral but important topic of the history of the marriage. "Let's start by going back to the beginning of all this. I'd like to get a brief history of your marriage. How did you two meet? One of you should begin telling me about it, and the other should speak up if you disagree with anything or want to add anything." This approach works if the parents are relatively calm and in control of themselves. If they begin arguing or interrupting, a more structured approach will have to be used, such as, "I am going to ask each of you questions and I would appreciate if the other did not interrupt. You will each have an opportunity to express your views, so please be courteous."

As the parents begin relating the history of the marriage, the evaluator is listening and taking notes, but is also watching the couple. Body language, little sounds of disagreement or agreement, and interjected comments all signal that the other parent is having reactions to what is said. It is important to let them contribute their input as the discussion goes along. All through the dialogue, the evaluator will be saying, "Do you agree with this, Mr. Jones?" "Ms. Jones, you shook your head. Do you have a different version of this?" The verbal interaction between them should be noted. Does one parent tend to dominate or interrupt the other? Does one continually defer or have trouble expressing his or her own viewpoint? Who seems to be the most clear-minded in relating the history? Who seems to be the most respectful of the other's right to have an opinion? Do the parents tend to agree on the sequence and nature of the events, or do they remember things so differently that they almost seem to live in two different realities? If the latter is the case, there is trouble ahead for the evaluation and for cooperative parenting in the future.

The questions suggested below assume that the couple has separated and has not yet divorced. The line of questioning would have to be modified if one of the litigants is not a parent, but rather is a grandparent, stepparent, or other.

—How long did you know each other before getting married?

—What attracted each of you to the other?

—When did problems begin in your marriage and what were the major ones?

—When (the first child) was born, what effect did it have on your relationship with each other?

—How did each of you take to parenting? Did either of you have difficulties adjusting to having a baby in the house? What kinds of difficulties?

—How did you two divide up the child-care responsibilities? (Get a detailed picture of who typically handled various tasks such as feeding, bathing, and getting up at night. Also get a good picture of how much time each parent spent with the child in an average day).

—As (the child) grew older, did your relationship with him or her change? How? What tasks of child care did each of you do? Who usually took him or her to school? Who helped with schoolwork?

—How did things change when the second child came (if relevant)? Ask some questions about parental involvement with each child.

—How were your parenting styles different? Did you ever argue about how to rear the children? (Get details here; what were each of their views on limit-setting, discipline, diet, school issues, socializing issues, and the like.)

—When did you two first decide to separate? Who actually left whom? Who moved out of the house and why?

—I want to get a very detailed picture of what the children's lives were like after the separation. (Questions here must be tailored to the individual family situation. With whom did the children stay at the time of separation? Did this change later? What was the pattern of contact with each parent? Was there a school change? How did each parent provide for the care of children? Were there new babysitters? These and similar facts will be especially important understanding the present feelings and needs of the children.)

—Tell me about each of your present situations now. (Where do each of them live? Where do they work? Is there a boyfriend or girlfriend in the picture? When does each parent see the children?)

—Now we get into some difficult territory, but it is important that we bring it out into the open. I am going to ask each of you to explain why you feel you should have custody of the children. If you have concerns about the other one's parenting, I want you to explain what those concerns are. I am going to ask each of you to wait until the other is completely finished before speaking, even though you will undoubtedly have strong feelings about what is being said. (If a parent has difficulty answering this open-ended question, more detailed questions should be asked, such as, "What living arrangement do you feel would be best for the children? In what ways do you think the children would benefit from living with you? What could you provide for them that the other parent could not? This includes emotional benefits as well as physical ones. Does the other parent do some things that you feel might be good for the child? How might the children suffer if they lived with the other parent?")

—If you should get custody of the children, what would be your plan for caring for them? That is, where would you and the children live?

Where would they go to school? What about daycare arrangements? (Each parent is asked this question).

—If you had custody of the children, how often would you like them to see the other parent? (This question is important because it gives indications about how supportive each parent is of the other's relationship with the children. For example, if a father feels that the children should visit their mother only once in a while, and only when they ask to visit, the evaluator should wonder whether this father is unconsciously trying to cut the mother out of the children's lives. If a mother comes up with a strange visitation plan that does not consider the children's needs, such as one year with her in New York and one year in Washington with the father, the evaluator questions her ability to make good judgments for the children.)

—If the other parent had custody, how often do you think the children should see you?

Naturally, the evaluator uses individual judgment as to how much time to spend on each question. The parents could take hours discussing any one topic, but the evaluator must try to extract the important information and move on to the next subject. The ideal length for this first interview is an hour and a half. This gives time to cover a great deal of territory, but does not exhaust the parents past the point of endurance. During the course of the evaluation, each parent must have the opportunity to talk to the evaluator alone. Certain subjects are more effectively discussed in the privacy of a one-to-one setting. An individual session (usually lasting an hour or less) can be scheduled at the office or can be incorporated into the home visit.

For evaluators with a counseling background, it is difficult to keep the joint interview from turning into a therapy session. Strong emotions arise, the parents may start to argue, one of them cries, old wounds are reopened. The evaluator may be tempted to let the parents go deeper into these feelings and to explore some of the underlying issues between them. But this temptation must be resisted. One cannot be an evaluator and a therapist at the same time.

Even if one could, there is not enough time to deal effectively with problems in the family. One can steer away from nonproductive involvement by following this rule: When a powerful emotion or issue arises in the session, acknowledge it, wait a few moments for the intensity of it to pass, and redirect the conversation back to concrete topics at hand. In practice, this may occur as follows:

Evaluator: Where did the children live after the separation?

    Father: With me. Joan walked out and left all three of us.

    Mother: What? How could you say that! "Joan walked out and left all three of us." It wasn't my choice to leave the children. The only way I could get out was to go myself. When I tried to take the children you wouldn't let me take them.

    Father: You never cared about those children. You only cared about yourself. You couldn't wait to get out and be "free." So great, just stay away and leave us alone.

    Mother: You bastard! This is so typical of you. No wonder I left! (mother starts to cry).

    Evaluator: All right. I am going to ask you both to stop for a few moments. We have gone far afield from my question. (fifteen seconds silence). I am only interested in where the children have been staying. I am not interested in whose fault anything is. Mr. Kenny, exactly how long did the children live at your house before they moved to Ms. Kenny's house?

If the parents still cannot recount the facts without getting upset, the issue is dropped for the time being and another, more neutral one is broached, such as, "Tell me how your son is doing in school right now." If one or both parents cannot respond to this redirecting, but keep getting overwhelmed by their own feelings, this is important to note because it says something about their emotional functioning.

Despite the stress involved, seeing parents together has distinct advantages. History-taking is economized by having both parties in the room at the same time. The discrepancies in their accounts can be dealt with immediately. When histories are taken separately, the evaluator often has to go back and forth between parents and check information. "Mr. Kenny, you said that the children stayed with you for two months. Ms. Kenny indicated that they were with you only for two weeks. Could you clarify this?" But more important, one gains invaluable information by observing the interaction between parties and comparing their personalities in each other's presence. Does one tend to provoke the other? Does one tend to focus on the needs of the children more consistently than the other? Is one individual calm and reasonable when alone with the evaluator but explosive and irrational when with the other parent? These and a host of other observations will help form a more complete picture of the family later on.

Interviewing Parents Separately

The following questions can be used to gain a more detailed picture of each parent's personal history. If the parties have been interviewed in joint session, some of the topics will already have been covered.

Childhood and Youth

Tell me about your own childhood. Where did you grow up? Who was in your family? What are some of the happiest memories you have from your childhood? Were there major problems in your family such as divorce, alcoholism, abuse, arrests (these should be asked about separately, such as "Did anyone in your family have a drinking problem?" Parents are reluctant to bring up negative things in their background unless asked specific questions). What kind of discipline did you get from your mother/father? Were you spanked or hit? Was a belt or other object used? What was your communication like with each of your parents? (or, "Were you more attached to one or the other?") What was the school experience like for you? How did you do in school? Did you have friends or were you more of a loner? What were your teenage years like? Did you and your parents have disagreements over issues such as curfew? Dating? School? Looking back, what was the greatest benefit to you of growing up in your family? What was the most negative thing?

Adulthood

After you left school, where did you go and what did you do? Tell me about your job history; what kinds of jobs have you had? What are you career goals? As an adult, have you had any problems with drinking? Drugs? Arrests? What about your brothers and sisters; how are they doing? Are they married, what jobs do they have, and so on. What kind of relationship do you have with your parents now? How often do you see them? What kind of involvement does your extended family have with your children? What do you know about your spouse's background?

MARRIAGE

How and when did you first meet your (ex)spouse? What attracted you to that person? What was your relationship with each other like before you married? Did it change after you married? What kinds of problems did you two have at first? Whose idea was it to have a baby? How did the pregnancy go, any problems? The birth? What were your feelings about being a new parent? What was hardest/easiest for you about being a parent? How did your spouse take to being a parent? How did you two share the child-care tasks? What were your schedules like; who was home with the child most of the time? How did you differ in your styles of parenting (diet, discipline, bedtime, and so on)? What are your views on discipline? Do you spank your children? How? How often on the average?

SEPARATION

When did the marriage begin to fall apart? Who left whom? Were either of you involved romantically with someone else?

Who moved out and who stayed in the home? Where did the children stay? Tell me in detail where the children have lived since the separation, and what their pattern of seeing each of you has been. What problems have you and your spouse had since the separation?

THE CHILDREN

Tell me about (first born) what kind of child is he or she? Did he or she have any physical problems as a baby? How about as he or she got older, any problems in school, with friends, with his or her parents? Do you feel that the child had been closer to one of you (parents) than the other? How has the child been affected by this separation? What do you think would most help the child get through this right now? Do you think the child has strong feelings about where he or she wants to live? (discuss other children).

CUSTODY

What living arrangements do you feel would be best for the children? Could this change in the future? How? (It is preferable to talk in terms of "living with" rather than "custody.") What do you feel you have to offer the children in terms of a good living environment, physically, emotionally, and intellectually? What is your best trait as a parent? In what areas do you think you need to improve? What concerns would you have if the children lived with the other parent in the future? When I ask your (ex)spouse that, what concerns or allegations will they tell me about you? If the children were living with you, what would be your plan for taking care of them? (Get details such as where the family would live, how the parent would support them, and what the daily routine would be like.) If the children lived with you, what visitation (or time-sharing) should they have with the other parent? What about holidays and vacation time? If the children lived with the other parent, what visitation should they have with you?

These are by no means the only questions to be asked, nor do all of them have to be asked. But they cover the important areas of concern. Later in the evaluation, there will be opportunities to learn more about some of these issues. The daily living environment of the children will be understood from the home visit, for example.

Because most parents have never been through an evaluation before, they do not know what to expect during the initial interview. The evaluator will continually have to steer them back to the important topics at hand, which all revolve around the best interests of the children. It is helpful for the evaluator to stress again and again that the children have needs of their own that may be different from the parents' wishes. The following conversation illustrates a form this may take:

Evaluator: What do you feel would be best for Tonya right now?

Parent: To live with me.

Evaluator: Why do you feel this would be best?

Parent: She belongs with me. I feel terrible since she has been gone. I haven't slept well and the house feels so empty.

Evaluator: So your need is to have her with you.

Parent: Yes.

Evaluator: I hear that. Now let's shift our focus for a moment and look at Tonya's needs. They may be different from yours.

Another exchange would be as follows:

Evaluator: You are the grandmother of the child, yet you are asking for custody. You must have concerns about Trevor living with his mother, or you wouldn't be involved in this court action.

Grandmother: I certainly do.

Evaluator: Tell me what concerns you have.

Grandmother: That girl (mother of the child) was always a problem. She's living with a man now and has no intentions of marrying him. I won't have anything to do with her as long as she lives like that.

Evaluator: You disapprove of her lifestyle.

Grandmother: I certainly do.

Evaluator: I hear that. But let's focus on Trevor. What do you feel he needs right now in a living situation?

By emphasizing the child orientation throughout the evaluation, litigants may learn to become somewhat more attuned to the important issues. Many litigants have never been encouraged to view things from this perspective. Later, when the final report comes out and discusses the findings from the standpoint of the children's best interests, they may be more prepared. Parents often come to the evaluation thinking that the case will be judged on the basis of which parent is more "deserving" to have the children. "This child came from my own body," a mother may say, "and I deserve to keep her." Or, "My ex-wife has had Jimmy for a full year. To be fair, I should have him for a year." Orienting the parent to the children's welfare can help eliminate some the this self-focused thinking. Of course, some individuals are so wrapped up in their own feelings that they cannot make the shift. They become annoyed if the evaluator forces them to talk about the children for very long. This is valuable information to note.

Throughout the interviews, the evaluator should take careful (but fast) notes. If the parent says something of importance, their words should be written down, verbatim, if possible. "If it weren't for that girlfriend he is living with, I'd let the kids live with him. They would do well at his house, if it weren't for that bitch." Having such statements on paper could be valuable later for writing the report, talking to attorneys, or testifying in court.

CONTINUING CASE STUDY
Norcross vs. Norcross

Both parents arrived on time for the joint interview. I gazed at them a moment before walking into the waiting room. Based on their appearances, one would not guess that they had ever been husband and wife. Mr. Norcross was clad in blue jeans, a casual short-sleeved shirt, and a visored hat that proclaimed "Caterpillar" in big green letters. Ms. Norcross, on the other hand, looked as though she were applying for an executive position with an oil company. Her wheat-colored linen suit and pale silk blouse contrasted attractively with the shiny black hair that brushed her shoulders.

Once we were seated in the office, I opened the session in the usual way. I commented that they probably did not enjoy coming to a joint meeting but that I appreciated their willingness to participate for the sake of the children. I added that although they were getting divorced, they would always be parents to Angelo and Lisa, and therefore would remain in some kind of relationship with each other all of their lives. At this point Ms. Norcross interjected, "You are aware, aren't you, that Lisa is my daughter from a previous relationship and is not subject to this action?" She had a low, beautiful voice and spoke like an attorney, I noted.

"Yes, I am. But Lisa and Mr. Norcross will not be dropping out of each other's lives, even though she is not his biological daughter. Later I want to talk to you about family relationships in more depth. Right now, I would like to understand the history of your relationship. Tell me, how did you first meet?

Six years ago, Ms. Norcross (then Ms. Beck) was living with her boyfriend, Cliff. The couple decided to have the yard landscaped. The landscaper who knocked on the door was Mr. Norcross. During the ten days it took to complete the job, the couple developed a warm relationship. Then Mr. Norcross decided to take a chance and ask her out for lunch the following week. She accepted, and within three weeks they were having an affair. After about two months, Ms. Beck moved out of Cliff's house and moved in with Mr. Norcross. She accidentally became pregnant almost immediately and the couple decided to marry shortly thereafter.

Although the father supplied a few details to this account, it was the mother who related most of the story. I wanted Mr. Norcross to participate more actively, so I asked him, "What was it that drew you to Ms. Norcross in the beginning?"

His eyes drifted away from us and he said to no one in particular, "I thought I had known a lot of women, but I never knew one like that, never one smart like she was, in the way she was. When she smiled at you it sort of took you into your own world." This odd little speech was spoken with such genuineness that I felt somewhat touched. I glanced over at Ms. Norcross, wondering whether she had any reaction to these words. But I could not tell from her face what she was feeling.

I realized that Lisa had never been mentioned in this account. Asking about the girl, I learned that she was living with her maternal grandmother during the time that Ms. Norcross and Cliff were together. The child was around two years old then. A year after Mr. and Ms. Norcross were married, Lisa came to live with them. There were many puzzles about all of this. Who was Lisa's father? Why did the girl live with her grandmother? Whose idea was it for her to rejoin the mother? What kind of relationship did Lisa and Mr. Norcross have? But I would have to wait until later for the answers. We still had much ground to cover in this interview.

"Let's move on to the time Angelo was born." I said. "What was it like for each of you having a new baby in the house?" My objective here was to determine how involved each of them was in the care of the baby, what their attitudes were, what problems they encountered, and so forth.

The mother began the narrative in her easy, flowing style. Because the couple was in love, I learned, the baby was heralded as the beginning of a wonderful new life together. Mr. Norcross was eager to attend the birth and participate in every aspect of the baby's care. Because he was working full time for the landscaping company, he could only be home on evenings and weekends. The mother did not work at this time. She had more freedom than many mothers with small infants, however, because several members of Mr. Norcross's family lived in town. They competed over who would take care of Angelo and Lisa. Thus both parents had many days and evenings away from the children.

After we talked about the children for a while I said, "Now we are going to get into difficult territory. I want to discuss the developments that led up to the separation. When did the marriage start running into trouble?"

"I wish I knew," Mr. Norcross said with unexpected intensity. "I wish I knew *why*." He stared at Ms. Norcross with a probing, slightly accusing look.

"Am I correct in assuming that you didn't want this divorce to take place, Mr. Norcross?" I asked.

"No, I didn't want it. We were good together. Why weren't you happy, Jenny? You never even told me why you weren't happy. You just up and left."

Ms. Norcross regarded him in silence. Then she turned to me and said, "I presume that you asked us to come here to talk about custody, not this."

"If you want to answer him briefly, that's all right, " I said, hating to leave Mr. Norcross hanging like that.

"No, I don't want to answer him. If he doesn't know the answer, then the answer will mean nothing."

"Let's move on, then." I said, seeing Mr. Norcross sigh and look away. "Let me ask you this: When did you two actually separate? Mr. Norcross, would you like to begin?"

He responded immediately. "One evening I came home from work and she was gone. Everyone was gone. There was no note. Her closet was empty. All the children's clothes were gone." He looked as stricken as if it had happened yesterday rather than four months ago.

"Did you want to add to the account, Ms. Norcross?"

"I wanted to do this as peacefully as possible, so I left while he was at work."

"Peaceful for who?" Mr. Norcross burst in. "What the hell did you think I would feel, finding you gone like that? And Angelo and Lisa gone, too, and all their little clothes gone. It took me more than a week to track her down, did you know that?" This last statement was addressed to me. "Would she ever have called me? Would I ever have seen the kids again?"

"I know this is upsetting for you, Mr. Norcross," I said. "Unfortunately, we cannot go into this right now. Later, you and I will have a chance to talk. Could you save it for then?

He shrugged and said, "Sure." I noted that although he was quick to become emotional, he could also step back from his feelings when it was appropriate to do so.

After Mr. Norcross had "tracked her down," he had asked to spend time with the children. The mother agreed as long as he promised not to try to talk to her when she brought them over. All visits took place at the father's house because the mother did not want him to know where she lived. There was no set pattern to these visits, but from what I could determine, the children would typically see him every three days or so. Sometimes they would stay from Thursday to Monday with the father. The paternal grandmother would watch Angelo on the weekdays while the father worked. Lisa would walk to school and walk home to the grandmother's house. The father would return, they would have dinner with grandmother, then go back to the house. This pattern appeared to work smoothly for about two months. Then the mother filed for divorce and asked for custody of Angelo. The father became extremely upset, retained a lawyer, and filed his own petition for custody. When the mother received these papers, she refused to bring the children to Mr. Norcross's house. The father called Ms. Gomez, who called Mr. Chappell. The attorneys helped the parents work out a temporary time-sharing plan until a custody evaluation could be completed. Basically, the children stay with Mr. Norcross every weekend from Friday afternoon until Monday morning, when he takes them to school or daycare. During the last three weeks, Lisa hasn't visited Mr. Norcross at all. Why, I wondered?

Little time was left in the session, so I zeroed in on the important topic of custody. "I would like to hear from each of you on what you feel you can offer Angelo as a custodial parent. You should talk to your attorney about what 'custodial parent' means in a legal sense. I would rather speak in terms of providing a home base for Angelo. Both of you will always be his parents, and he should spend high quality time at each household. But this evaluation will recommend that one of you provide Angelo with a home base. Mr. Norcross, perhaps you could begin.

The father looked at his hands and said nothing. The only sound in the room was the suddenly audible ticking of the clock. A small smile crossed Ms. Norcross's lips that I was unable to interpret. I was about to ask Mr. Norcross some questions to help him express himself, when he finally spoke.

"Well, that's a hard one. I don't want to take Angelo away from his mother, don't get me wrong. But I gave it a lot of thinking. Angelo needs to be loved in a big way and I can do that. Everybody in my family loves Angelo. They love each other, too, and they just plain love kids. Jenny isn't as much that way. She can be warm and cold. Mostly cold."

"Let me see if I understand what you're saying," I said. "You feel that you can provide Angelo with the loving home that he needs. You think he will also benefit from the love that your relatives give him. You are not so sure that his mother can provide this as well."

"Yes, that's exactly what I said," the father answered, looking pleased.

"Ms. Norcross, what do you feel you can offer Angelo?"

"As you know," she began without hesitation, "there is a lot more to a child's rearing than love. I love Angelo as much or more than anyone does. But I am also aware of his other needs. He needs intellectual stimulation; he needs good adult role models who have reached some degree of self realization themselves; he needs to explore the world and all its excitement. I believe I can provide these things much better than his father can. I know Jacob loves Angelo, but his world is limited. As for his relatives, they smother the boy."

"Smother him!" the father exclaimed, jumping up from his chair, "They are crazy about him and he eats it up!"

"Well," I said, standing up also, "I'm afraid our time is up for this session. I want to thank the both of you for sharing so much information. You were both very cooperative. I'll be calling each of you for individual appointments. There is a great deal more to discuss. Also, we will be making arrangements for a home visit to each of your homes." The mother shook my hand and whisked out of the room, taking her faintly perfumed aura with her. Mr. Norcross stood looking after her with sad eyes.

Individual Interviews

JENNIFER NORCROSS

After the joint interview, I was left with more questions than answers about Ms. Norcross's past. I used the private session to focus on her personal history; I realized that I had never asked her what drew her to Mr. Norcross. The dissimilarity between the two still struck me as unusual. I also wanted to talk about the children more with her. The home visit would provide most of the data on this, however.

The interview passed quickly. Here is a summary of what I learned:

Jennifer reported that her family moved at least every two years as she was growing up. She attributed this to her father's restlessness. He would start up a business, wait until it became fairly successful, then become bored with it, sell it, and announce, "I think we should move to California!" or some other region. This caused many arguments in the family. Jennifer's mother and older sister complained continually. Jennifer herself reports that she did not mind the moves and found it rather exciting. She always made new friends easily and forgot them just as easily when she left. When she was 13 years old, her mother and father got a divorce. Jennifer is still not clear about what happened because the father disappeared out of their lives for years and the mother would never talk about it. She suspects that her father was involved with another woman because he remarried a few months after the divorce. He did keep up his child support obligations, however.

At 17, Jennifer went to a state college a hundred miles from her home. Rather than live in the dormitory, she moved in with a boyfriend four years her senior. He went home for the summer, but she decided to stay there and obtained a job as a receptionist with a young dentist. She and the dentist became involved (he was married) and they carried on this relationship through the summer and into the fall semester. When her boyfriend returned, he was surprised at her situation but withdrew from the scene and did not cause trouble.

A few months later, Jennifer met a graduate student in one of her classes and began dating him. She was becoming annoyed with the restrictions on the relationship with her married doctor, so she said goodbye to him. Soon she and her graduate student moved into his apartment together. Jennifer remembers this as one of her best years because they shared many intellectual and cultural activities together. It was he who introduced her to the field of psychology, and she decided to make this her major. This relationship ended suddenly and unhappily for Jennifer. Her boyfriend had been acting strangely for about six weeks. He kept telling her that he had begun therapy at the university counseling center, but would not discuss the content of the sessions. One evening he took her out to a Chinese restaurant and announced that he was gay. Even though their sexual relations had been good, he had realized that his essential nature was not heterosexual and that he had been hiding from himself for years. He now wanted to pursue a lifestyle that was more genuine, and that meant saying goodbye to her. Jennifer reported that she felt more unhappiness over this than over any relationship before or since.

Jennifer dropped out of school at the end of the term and moved to another state. She had a series of relationships and a series of jobs. When she was proposed to by Carl Beck, an affluent contractor, she accepted. She became pregnant with Lisa almost immediately. A year after the child was born, Jennifer found that she was bored with the marriage and left the house, taking the child with her. She moved back to her mother's town and lived with her for six months. She then met Cliff, a business man, who lived in Colorado. They began a relationship and she decided to move here with him. The grandmother suggested that Lisa stay with her, and this was agreeable.

After eight months of living with Cliff, Jennifer met Jacob Norcross. What attracted her to him? He seemed sweet, earnest, vulnerable. He was two years younger than she, but seemed ten years younger at times. Yet she enjoyed him. Jennifer knew that he was not her intellectual equal, but that didn't matter at first. He knocked himself out trying to please her. She thought it would be a nice experience to live with him for a time. If she had not gotten pregnant, she probably would not have married him. She had to admit that he was terrific with the baby. In fact, he loved children, probably because he was a child himself in many ways. It was his idea to bring Lisa back to live with them.

Everything worked well for about two years. But Jennifer began realizing how mismatched they were. His cultural level was low. He would come home from landscaping with dirt-encrusted fingernails and filthy clothes, get a beer, flop down on the couch, and watch television. The couple had nothing in common to talk about. She started feeling that she wanted to go back to school. He was not supportive of this at all. When she enrolled in two university courses, the trouble began. He questioned her incessantly about what men were in the class, whom she talked to each day, and where she went after school in the evenings. She became defiant and brought male friends home after class. Jacob would glower and leave the room. She became increasingly frustrated at his standing in the way of her progress. Finally, she decided to leave one day. Since then, she has not experienced a moment's regret, she reported.

At present, Jennifer lives in an apartment near the campus. She is dating a graduate student in psychology named William, but she is not serious about him. It will be a long time before she is ready for another serious relationship, she emphasized.

Regarding the children, Jennifer believes that Lisa is drifting away from Jacob as time goes by. For the last several weekends she has not shown much interest in going to his house. But the child is becoming quite attached to Phillip, Jennifer added. Jennifer welcomes this development, because she does not think Jacob is a good long-term influence on either child. The role model of a father and of a man that he presents is inadequate. He lacks personal ambition and has little interest in anything outside of his immediate family and friends. He has also had a drinking problem in the past that could flare up again now that he is alone. The influence of Jacob's mother and father is really not good for Angelo in the long run, Jennifer believes. If Angelo grows up in that family, he will turn into a dull, beer-drinking worker just like his father.

Individual Interview

JACOB NORCROSS

In the individual session, Jacob was more relaxed and expressive. He still seemed to have difficulty summarizing information or relating long sequences of events. I therefore had to ask him many questions about his childhood and adult years.

Jacob's family moved here when he was five years old, and they have lived in the same house ever since. His father owns a small nursery and does part-time landscaping. From the time they were eight or nine years old, Jacob and his two older brothers assisted their father in this business. Childhood memories seem to be primarily happy ones. The four males spent a lot of time outdoors and went hunting and fishing in their spare time. Regarding their mother, "We treated her like gold. We loved her a lot. Anyway, our father would have kicked our little butts if we didn't treat her right." I asked him how he and his brothers were disciplined. Were they hit, for example? He could remember being spanked only a few times when he was little. But his father would raise his big hand (big enough to reach two full octaves on the old piano, Jacob added) and "scare the hell of us boys if we got rowdy." I asked how Jacob usually disciplined Angelo. "I look at him real stern and say in a bear voice, 'Angelo!' and he stops whatever he is doing," he replied. Asked if he has ever had to spank Angelo, he said, no and hoped that he never would.

Did he have any unhappy memories of his childhood? Yes, and it was one big, long, unhappy memory: school. From the first grade on, he had problems with words and with reading. By the third grade, he used to start to cry if he saw a book. He repeated the third grade. In fifth grade the school got him a special tutor, and that helped some. But junior high and high school were very hard. The only subjects he did well in were math, shop, and physical education. He just barely graduated. Jacob said that one of his biggest fears is that Angelo will have the same kind of problem he did. The boy seemed smart so far, "but reading seems to be separate from smartness," Jacob felt. I asked him what he would do if he discovered that Angelo had this problem. He said, "I would get him help right away, before he gets covered over with misery the way I did. I would pay money to get him a special tutor and would be on that school's case day and night if they didn't do something for him."

After high school, Jacob got a job with a landscaping company. He and his family thought it would be better to work outside of his father's business. Also, the father could not afford to pay him a full wage. Jacob liked his job and held it for a year and six months until the company went out of business. Then he worked for a stone and rock supply outfit for eight months. Finally, a job opened up with another landscaping company and he took it. He has worked there for almost six years. He makes fairly good money except for the winter months, when he works in the nursery and makes less. Asked about his plans for the future, he said that he would like to have his own landscaping business someday. He knows quite a few people who like his work and he thinks that he could make a go of it. But it is risky financially and he wants to build up a better customer base before he quits his job.

I asked Jacob about his relationships with women before he met Ms. Norcross. He looked a little embarrassed and said that there were not all that many women. He had a steady girlfriend during his last two years of high school. The next fall, she went off to college. She wrote two letters; then he never heard from her again. He dated girls now and then for about a year and a half. Then he met Jennifer on that landscaping job. He said again how she was the most remarkable woman he had ever come across. He believes that he fell in love with her within the first hour of talking to her. He knew that she was living with another man, but he figured that all was fair in love and war, and he decided to pursue her. When she eventually left Cliff to live with him, he was the happiest man in the world. The pregnancy was a surprise but he was happy about it. He urged her to marry him.

Jennifer never seemed fond of his family and told him so often. In her angry moments she called them "dumb Italians." This made him angry but he never could stay mad long at anyone, especially at someone as beautiful as she. The best year they spent was right after the baby was born. She seemed to depend on him a great deal and was grateful when he would take the baby for a day so that she could go out. She even began to be nicer to his family because they were so anxious to help out the couple and babysit.

I told Jacob that this was a bit off the subject, but that I was curious about the name "Norcross." It was not Italian. What was the story behind it? He said that no one has been able to figure out who this original Norcross was. He was an immigrant who came to Italy at least a 150 years ago and married an Italian woman. Jacob's family, all Italians, has always been a little ashamed of the name.

I asked how Lisa came to live with Jennifer, Angelo, and him. Jacob said that he never could quite understand why Lisa was living in another state with the grandmother. He began to feel bad, as though the three of them were a happy family but one little girl had been sent away. He had met Lisa on a trip to the grandmother's and she was a dear child. After discussing it for a few months, Jennifer agreed to have Lisa live with them. The girl was three years old at this time. After Lisa came, however, she did not seem happy. She missed her grandmother a lot and cried for her. She appeared to be jealous of the baby and sometimes did bad things to him such as pouring milk on his head. One time, she smeared peanut butter all over his bottom and then said that he needed his diaper changed. Jennifer never seemed concerned about all of this, but would just say that Lisa would adjust in time. Jennifer sort of ignored Lisa, in Jacob's opinion. The girl could say, "Mommy, mommy," a dozen times and the mother still would not answer her. He told himself that Jennifer had studied psychology and knew about children. But it worries him now because he thinks that Jennifer does not really care about the children as much as she cares about herself. He also thinks that she is "man crazy" because she has had so many lovers. He fears that she will find another boyfriend soon; in fact, he is pretty sure that she already has one, some blond guy from the university. Lisa and Angelo have both mentioned a fellow kissing mommy. It makes Jacob angry and jealous and he has a hard time not thinking about it all of the time.

"What would your fears be if Jennifer were awarded custody of Angelo?" I asked. Given that he was more relaxed now, I thought that I might get a fuller answer than I had gotten in the joint interview. "I don't think she would ever hurt Angelo," he said. "But she isn't fixed on him, you know what I mean? He is just there to her. My fears for him? That he'll grow up like one of those plants that gets just enough light and just enough food to keep living. But when you look close at it, you see that it never grew to what it should be."

4

The Home Visit

Strangely enough, professionals in private practice generally neglect one of most important aspects of an evaluation: the home visit. Most custody studies take place entirely in an office setting. Crucial information is thereby lost. Seeing parents and children together in the intimacy of their home setting provides a perspective on the case that cannot be duplicated elsewhere. Observing firsthand the physical, social, and emotional environments that each parent offers the children can sometimes be a determining factor of the evaluation.

Because many mental health professionals have never had occasion to undertake a home visit, this discussion will include basic consideration that the experienced caseworker may find familiar.

What attitude does one assume when approaching the door of a parent's home? As simple as this sounds, it can be problematic. For example, do we take the stance of a tough, investigative researcher who is endeavoring to uncover all the "dirt"? If so, perhaps we will spring a surprise visit and catch the parent unaware. We will maintain solemn expressions on our faces, will decline a cup of coffee, and will not engage in chitchat. At the other extreme, we can picture ourselves as a friendly guest. We will work hard to put everyone at ease, will stay for dinner, and may even ask for a recipe.

Obviously, neither of these approaches are satisfactory. The first one is wrong because the evaluator is not trying to "nail" anybody. His or her only purpose is to understand the entire family better and to evaluate how each side of the family is able to meet the child's needs. Surprise attacks in the form of unannounced visits would be more distasteful and traumatic for the evaluator than for the parent. They would also be foolishly time consuming because one may arrive only to find that nobody is home. On the other hand, one is not a guest in the ordinary sense of the word. The home visit is an organized extension of the information-gathering process. If one decides to have a meal at the house (and this can be a valuable experience), it is only to observe family interaction in a special setting. A good policy to follow is to be warm and at ease, but to keep control of the situation by structuring the course of events. Everyone then stays focused on the purpose of the visit.

When the appointment is made, it should be emphasized that all household members must be home at the time of the visit. This includes persons who may not be in the family but who live in the house. An aunt, roommate, or live-in lover could be an important figure in the child's life, for better or worse. Knowing in advance who must be interviewed enables one to plan ahead. It will make a difference, for example, whether the evaluator will be visiting a mother and her infant only, or will be encountering an extended family household of 13 members. If the children have not been seen previously in an office interview, the parents should be instructed to tell the children about the scheduled visit, to explain that the evaluator is trying to understand the family so that good decisions can be made about the children, and to let the children know that the evaluator will be talking to each of them alone.

Initiating the Family Session

Generally the whole family is milling around waiting for the evaluator to arrive. Those individuals who tend toward manipulativeness may stage a sparkling "family interaction" to take place right when the visitor enters. One family, I recall, could be seen through the curtains sitting quietly in chairs as I approached the house. Just as I knocked on the door, they sprang into action. The stepmother and daughter began shuffling a deck of cards while the father and son batted furiously at a hockey game set in the living room. "It looks like you are all having fun," I commented as I walked in, and they were immensely pleased.

The first 30 to 45 minutes of the visit is a good time to talk to everyone together and to observe family interaction. The evaluator can provide the proper focus by reviewing for everyone again the purpose of the visit, that is, to see where the children live, to meet everyone in the household, to get a sense of what the family does together, and to see what the children's daily routine is like. General questions may be addressed to the family to get them involved in a family discussion. Among these are:

—If I weren't here today, tell me what each of you would be doing right now. What is a typical (Saturday, Thursday afternoon, and so on) like for your family?

—What activities do you most enjoy doing together as a family?

—How does your family divide up the workload around the house? (To the children:) Do each of you have special chores or duties that you must do? What happens if you don't do them?

—Every family has times when they don't get along with each other. What kinds of problems do you have? (Or, to the children:) Do you ever have disagreements with each other? With your parents? What do you disagree about? When problems come up, how do you handle them?

—To help me understand your family, let's play a game. It's more than a game because it has to do with feelings. I would like each of you to pick one person in your family and name the thing you like best about him or her and then name one thing you would like to change about him or her.

These are only a few of the approaches that will help a family begin talking. The evaluator is interested in the information that comes to light, but is even more interested in the patterns of interaction taking place among family members. Who sits near whom? Does the parent tend to direct his or her attention to one child more often than another? Do the adults give the children a chance to express opinions freely? Do the children seem open and spontaneous in sharing feelings around a parent? Do the children support each other's input, or are they competitive and disruptive with each other? Does it seem that this family has often had discussions together, or is it like pulling teeth to get them to engage in a cooperative conversation? Is there laughter and sense of joy between them? Observing factors like these will add a great deal to one's knowledge of the family. It will also be extremely valuable to compare the family interaction at one household with the family interaction at the other. Do the children seem equally comfortable in both places? Does one child's behavior seem different (e.g. more open, more closed, more physically lively, more affectionate) in the presence of a particular parent or home setting? How do the parents compare in their ability to relate to the children?

It is often helpful to have the family participate in an activity that is not verbal, especially when young children are involved. Among the techniques that could be used are the following:

(1) Ask the parent and child(ren) to build cooperatively a structure out of blocks or Legos. They have about ten minutes to complete it. (You may have to come prepared with your own blocks or Legos for this.) Sit back and watch them. Who initiates the activity? What role does the parent assume with the children? Parents may take over and start telling the child how to build the structure; parents may sit passively and let the child do most of it; or they may interact cooperatively with the child. Do family members tie into each other's activities, or do they each build their own separate parts then try to put them together? Do they seem to enjoy working together? Are they competitive? Do older children help younger children? Is someone left out? These and a host of other observations will tie other data gathered in the study.

(2) Give the parent and child(ren) a large piece of paper, crayons, and pencils and ask them to draw a joint picture together. Give them about ten minutes. Who suggests the subject matter of the picture? Can family members agree right away, or do they dispute over it? Does the parent let the child participate in his or her own way, or is the child's behavior continually being directed? Is the parent critical of the child's drawing? Can the family members really build on each other's input? Or do they each do their own thing on different parts of the paper?

(3) Ask family members to draw cooperatively a picture of their family. Who chooses to draw which family members (e.g., the son says, "Let me draw Daddy!")? This may reflect attachments. Is the separated spouse included in the picture? Who suggested that he or she be there? In the final product, who is depicted next to whom? What is the family doing in the picture? Any of these observations could be reflective of more general patterns in the family.

(4) As a verbal addition to the above technique, family members are asked to take the family drawing and add dialogue. Each person in the drawing is depicted as saying something. The words are written above their heads, cartoon style. (See Figure 4.1 for example drawing.)

Some children are too young to participate in any of these exercises. In this case, parent-child interaction is observed while carrying on a conversation with the parent. The evaluator may ask the parent about the child's habits, schedule, problems, and development. Some of this will have been covered during the office interviews. During the home visit, the tone of the conversation will generally be lighter and more casual. Does the baby have a good appetite? What does your child like to play with? How often does he take naps? When did your daughter learn to walk? How does your son get along with the dog? Meanwhile, everything is being observed. Can the parent interact with the evaluator and yet attend

NOTE: As the boy's picture and captions indicate, he perceives chaotic and un-supportive relationships in his family. The evaluator wrote in the identification of family members.

Figure 4.1 A 10-Year-Old Boy's Drawing of His Family

to the children, or does the parent get so wrapped up in conversation that the toddler wanders out of the door? How do parents respond when the child starts to cry or pulls on their shirt, wanting something? Can the adult set limits on the child and then stick to them? Does the parent seem practiced and comfortable in changing the baby's diaper and attending to the dozens of required child-care tasks? Is there an affectionate, heartfelt acceptance for the child's everyday actions? I remember a teenage mother who, when her 10-month-old baby spit baby-food all over the two of us, exclaimed with a delighted laugh, "My, my, what a messy eater!"

Spending Time with the Children

After the family session, the evaluator will want to interview each child individually. An easy way to initiate this session is to say directly to the child, "I would like to spend a little time with just you alone. Could we go to your room? You can show me some of your special things." Children enjoy talking about their favorite toys and possessions. In the safety and familiarity of their own room, youngsters generally feel at ease, even with a stranger. How the evaluator works with the child at this point will be covered in the next chapter. The important consideration here is making the most of being in the child's home environment. Look around the room. Has an effort been made to create a cheerful, comfortable setting? Even if the family has little money, this can be evaluated. Perhaps there are hand-drawn pictures tacked on the wall to brighten things up. How does the child's room compare with other rooms in the house? Is the parent's bedroom a showplace but the child's room bleak? Glance at the child's supply of clothes. Has care been devoted to them? What about toys and books. Do the playthings seem appropriate for the child's age? Are the books well used, suggesting that the child frequently reads or is read to by a parent? Does the room appear to have been kept relatively clean, or has everything been thrown hastily into the closet into a big heap?

Where is the child's room located in relation to the rest of the family? Is it stuck down a steep flight of stairs in the basement so that a parent would not be able to hear the child call out at night? Or has the child been given the nicest bedroom in the house?

Each child should have a private, separate session, even if sharing the same room. Occasionally a child, particularly an older one, will appear to be so concerned about privacy that he or she is not able to communicate effectively. The child may look around, make sure that the door is shut, or whisper. In this case, the evaluator should consider going outside with the child. Walking around in the yard or taking a short walk down the street could provide a greater sense of security. This behavior should also be noted for future reference and an effort should be made to understand why the child is so anxious and fearful.

The objects in a child's room provide a good launching point for conversation.

Evaluator: Tell me, Megan, what is your favorite thing in this room?

Child: This little dog who lives in the basket.

Evaluator: It's cute. Where did you get it?

Child: My Grampa gave it to me.

Evaluator: Sounds like your Grampa is a nice man.

Child: He is. My mom and I always go to see him on Sunday. He tells me stories and is nice. He has a dog just like this one. But his dog is real.

Evaluator: Now let's see, you have another grampa, don't you? The one on your Dad's side of the family?

Child: Yes, but I've never been to his house. He lives far away. I think he might be mean but I'm not sure.

From this short exchange, we have learned that Megan has a significant attachment to her maternal grandfather. When a child identifies an object as the favorite, it usually has personal meaning beyond the item itself. We also learned that she has had no interaction with her paternal grandfather and must have heard negative things about him—from whom? Does she have contact with anyone in the father's extended family? The extended network of family support for a child is always important to assess.

Remember that a second opportunity will be available to interview the child at the other home. Therefore everything does not have to be accomplished in one sitting. Around 45 minutes alone with the child at each home visit is usually adequate. Some evaluators prefer to interview the children privately in their office playrooms. In this case, the time spent in the child's room can be reduced.

At some point during the evaluation, all siblings should be seen together, without a parent present. Depending on the children's ages, they may be encouraged to build something out of blocks, play a board game, or share opinions on an interesting topic. This will provide an opportunity to witness their interaction with each other. Are they respectful of each other's space, or do they try to overrun each other? Do they seem cooperative or competitive? Does one dominate the others? Who seems to take care of whom? Do they all participate, or is one child isolated? Have the siblings "taken sides" in the custody dispute, defending one parent and condemning the other?

After the work with individual children is finished, the family may be addressed as a whole again. If such information has not come to light earlier, this is a good time to get a clear picture of the children's activity patterns as they relate to the home environment. Where is the school? How do they get there each day? Where do their friends live? What is the neighborhood like in terms of busy streets, parks, and social environment? This is also a good time to tour the house, if this has not been done. Careful notes should be taken on the physical characteristics of the house, particularly if one does not have a good memory for those kinds of things. I have been embarrassed on the witness stand more than once because I could not answer the simple question, "Exactly how many rooms does the mother's house have?"

Evaluator or Sanitation Inspector?

When parents learn that the evaluator will visit the home, the first thing they usually plan is to clean up the house. An anxious parent may invite the evaluator to inspect closets and cabinets. Naturally there is no need to do this. It is helpful at this point to remind everyone of the purpose of the visit: to understand the family better by getting to know them in their natural home setting. This usually puts parents at greater ease.

As long as a home is tolerably in order, no more attention has to be paid to the matter. There are exceptions to this. Sometimes the cleanliness of the house is an issue in the custody dispute. If one parent has alleged that the other lets the children live in an unhealthy physical environment, this should be investigated. Some people encourage the evaluator to "see the true situation" by making an unannounced visit. For reasons stated before, this is not a good idea. It is also unnecessary, for a house that is chronically dirty will remain so, even after a crash straightening job is launched. The layers of dirt, piles of debris, stained walls, and unwholesome smell will still be in evidence. Interviews with neighbors or professionals who may have visited the house (such as a social worker) can also shed light on the customary condition of the home. Interviews with older children supply additional clues. In reality, those parents who are unable to maintain an adequate level of household care are usually unable to mobilize the effort necessary to "put on a good appearance" for the evaluator. So a deteriorated home environment will probably appear just that way at the time of the visit.

All homes should be screened for obvious health hazards such as debris in the yard or house, unsanitary kitchen or bathroom conditions, dangerous space heaters or fireplaces, broken windows, leaking ceilings, and other substandard conditions. A parent's awareness of child-safety issued can be gauged by noting precautions they have taken. One mother spoke contemptuously about how messy the father's house always was, emphasizing that her neater apartment provided a much better environment for their two-year-old son. Upon visiting both homes, it was observed that the mother's residence was indeed much neater than that of the father's. But her second story apartment opened onto a porch with only a single thin board for a railing. Given one careless moment, the child could have tumbled two stories to the cement below. The fact that the mother had lived there four months without becoming concerned about this reflected something about her lack of awareness.

Housekeeping styles and habits are often strongly influenced by socioeconomic background. Acceptable levels of orderliness for one group may be unacceptable for another. The evaluator should remember that the litigants' home environments are being compared only against each other, not against an ideal standard. Both living situations may be below par (or perhaps superior to the evaluator's own!), but what difference does it make? For this child, the only options available are the environments offered by each litigant. The rare exception to this is when each litigant's situation presents such hazards to the child's well being that a state agency should be contacted.

Staying for Lunch or Dinner

If it can be arranged, planning to have lunch or dinner at a parent's home is always a valuable experience. Parents usually welcome this opportunity because it affords a more informal setting than does the serious, structured office context. The evaluator should make sure, however, that both litigants have the opportunity to have a home visit around mealtime.

Information on the family's nutritional habits (which is often an issue in custody litigation) can be gathered in the context of a meal. Noting what kinds of foods are around the kitchen and what is served at the meal is a beginning point. Does the focus seem to be on natural, low-sugar foods, or are there boxes of cookies, snack-cakes, and sweet cereals about? Do the children drink milk or soft drinks with the meal? This is a good time to ask the parents what they like to cook. The children can be asked, "Name me some the foods that your mom cooks for you" or, "Who can tell me what you had for dinner last night? Do you remember what you had for dinner the night before?" "Do you take vitamins?" "Do you ever go out to eat? Where do you usually go?" Questions pertaining to sharing of household tasks can also be asked in this natural setting. "Do you ever help your dad cook?" "Who usually sets the table? Who cleans up? Do you ever have disagreements about this?"

Family interaction during a meal is a goldmine of information. Who sits by whom at the table? Does this pattern fit with the pattern observed in the living room? For example, does one child always seem to be near the parent, whereas the other child seems more isolated? Do the siblings prefer each other to the parent? Who helps the little children get served—the adult or an older sibling? Does the parent keep an eye on the children to make sure that they have everything they need? Does the family eat in isolated silence, broken only by the evaluator's voice, or do they have a natural, warm way of interacting? How does the parent handle problems at the table, such as two children squabbling over the potato chips? If a child refuses to eat, or becomes demanding, how does the parent respond? Generally, does mealtime tend to generate tension for this family? These and similar observations can be compared with patterns seen in the other household.

Last Considerations

To keep the evaluation as balanced as possible, home visits to each of the litigants should have parallel structures. If one home is visited on a Saturday mid-morning when everyone is relaxed, the other should not be visited on a Thursday after school and work when everyone is tired. If a meal is planned at one home, it should be planned at the other. Family sessions should last about the same amount of time at each residence, and similar though not identical techniques should be used.

When the report is written, specific observations from the home visit may often be included. If the report did not favor a parent, the parent may object later that the evaluator misinterpreted what was going on, or failed to take into account the fact that the children were cranky, tired, or upset because of the evaluation. "You stated in the report that Kristin seemed withdrawn and noncommunicative with her mother at home," an attorney may say. "Of course she was withdrawn that day. Didn't you know that she was coming down with the flu?" Therefore, the evaluator should be careful to ask the parents about any unusual conditions at the time of visit. "Is it time for the baby's nap? When does she usually fall asleep?" "Is Michael feeling well today? Any colds or anything?" "You told Heather about my coming here today. How did she seem to feel about it? Do you think she is upset?" "This is sometimes a hard time for kids, right before dinner. Do they seem more agitated than usual?" In this way, parents are aware that the evaluator is taking into consideration the various factors that may be influencing a child's behavior.

Because the home visit represents a warmer, more informal contact, parents sometimes feel like opening up emotionally to the evaluator. This may be appropriate and useful for discussing issues that are directly relevant to the case. In fact, the last 20 minutes or so of the home visit usually should be spent with the parent alone as a way of wrapping up the event. The evaluator may ask, "Are there other things about the children that you wish to share?" "Is there anything else about your home environment here that I might not have asked you about, but that you feel I should know?" Questions such as these provide an opportunity for the parent to bring up issues that might have been neglected. Parents also may use this opportunity to discuss their concerns about the other parent further, or to relate recent problems between the litigants. I always cast a glance around to make sure that the children are out of earshot for these discussions. It is also valuable to note whether the parent is sensitive enough to stop talking about these topics if a child comes into the room.

Throughout these discussions, the evaluator makes sure that the interaction does not gravitate toward a counseling session. Parents may want to discuss at length their lonely feelings since the separation, their poor relationship with their in-laws, their new love affair, and other topics that cannot be explored satisfactorily in the context of an evaluation. Unless this input has direct relevance for understanding the custody case, it is best to redirect the conversation back to the welfare of the children.

CONTINUING CASE STUDY
Norcross vs. Norcross

Because I interviewed the mother first in the individual session, I decided to visit the father's home first. I have found that one's impressions may be influenced in a small way by the order in which one receives information. Therefore I try to stagger my interviews so that no one parent is always seen first.

Home Visit—Jacob Norcross

Jacob lived in the house that the couple shared before the separation. It was a petite structure of white wood with a gable over the door, giving it a gingerbread-house look. The yard was beautifully landscaped with tiers of purple and yellow flowers rising to the level of the windows. Driving down the street, I noticed that most of the houses in the neighborhood did not measure up to those standards. They tended to be run down and shabby looking. The lawn across the street was decorated with old car engines and various massacred machines.

Jacob greeted me at the door. A tiny face with dark oversized eyes peeked out from behind the father's legs. "This must be Angelo," I smiled. We sat in big, somewhat worn easy chairs in the living room. Jacob said that Lisa had not wanted to visit him that day. (I told him that Lisa did not have to be there because she was not officially part of his household, but that it was fine if she did come.) This worried him because she had not visited for weeks. They used to be very close, he said. He suspected that the mother was discouraging her from seeing him.

I wanted to focus in on Angelo. Jacob and I discussed the boy's schedule, likes and dislikes, eating habits, friends in the neighborhood, and preschool. While we talked, I watched the father and child interact. Angelo had a whole battalion of trucks and cars. He raced them from one end of the living room to the other, emitting throaty roaring noises as he went. The father winced slightly and paused when the sound over-whelmed his conversation, but he did not seem to mind the boy's fun. Fortunately for my own eardrums, Angelo decided that he was hungry and temporarily abandoned his racetrack. "I'm hungry, dad!" he announced.

"What do you want, kid?" Jacob said, sweeping him into his lap.

"A Fudgesicle!"

"You can't have a Fudgesicle today. I'm out. How about an Eskimo Pie?" Soon Angelo was happily smeared in chocolate.

"What kinds of snacks does Angelo usually eat?" I asked.

"Oh, he likes ice cream, donuts, Twinkies. You name it, he likes it."

When Angelo finished his snack, I told the father that I would like to watch him and Angelo play together for a little while. I had brought with me some large-sized Legos (I know Angelo was too young for the tiny Legos) and I wanted them to build something together. It didn't matter what they built. They had about ten minutes. Jacob dumped out the Legos on the floor and waited for Angelo to grab a few. "You know how those fit together. You played with them at Aunt Rose's house." The boy stuck some pieces together. Jacob selected a big flat piece to use as a base. "Do you think your contraption will fit on here?" he said. The boy stuck it on. "What is it, anyway?" the father asked.

"A dump truck."

"Great, a dump truck. Let's put a winch on it." They proceeded like this for awhile until they had a truck that might have originated from another planet. Angelo obviously loved it.

It was time for lunch. Jacob was pleased when I had told him that I would like to have lunch there if possible. He had set the table in advance. "I hope you like tuna fish sandwiches," he called from the kitchen.

"That sounds fine," I answered.

The table was laden with a big bowl of potato chips, a quart-sized bottle of Pepsi, and carrot sticks. Jacob then appeared from the kitchen with four tuna fish sandwiches stacked between his hands. "One for each of us," he said, plopping a sandwich down on each plate, "and one extra," which he put on a napkin in the middle of the table. "Do you say grace?" he said.

"I want to do whatever you usually do here," I answered.

"You say it, Angelo," the father said. Then the boy recited a soft little litany.

"Angelo," I said, "is your dad a good cook?" (Kids always say yes).

"Yep!" he said.

"What is your favorite thing that he cooks?"

"Hamburgers."

"Ah, hamburgers. Mr. Norcross, what else do you like to cook?"

"Well, I do a lot with Hamburger Helper. We have steaks sometimes. I just learned how to cook porkchops. I get enough pasta at my Mom's, so I don't cook that."

"Did you do any cooking during the marriage?"

"No, Jennifer did all of that and we also ate a lot at my folks'. The truth is, I'm actually just learning how to cook. My sister is helping me."

After lunch, I said that I wanted to spend some time with Angelo alone. We went into his bedroom, a small, narrow room that seemed a little barren. Few toys, clothes, or decorations were in evidence. Only a sheet covered the bed. "Is this the bed where you sleep?" I asked, unable to think of anything else to ask about for the moment.

"Yep. Sometimes I sleep with my dad."

"What is your favorite thing in this room?"

"Well, okay, but it's in the closet, and my dad said not to show you in the closet because, now, *that's* a mess!"

"That's all right. Closets are messy sometimes."

He opened the door and I saw toys, broken boxes from old games, and various socks, little shirts, and other articles of clothing tangled up together in the corner. Angelo reached into the heap and miraculously extricated a rusty dump truck. He proudly held against my nose to see.

"Wow, what a truck. Who gave it to you?"

"Santa Claus, when I was a baby."

"You like this truck better than all your other toys."

"Yep."

"Tell me, what makes this truck your favorite thing?"

"Cause it goes fast," he said, losing interest in my foolish questions and racing the vehicle through the air with a roar. This was going nowhere, so I devoted the rest of the session to the structured fantasy games I had prepared.

After about 40 minutes, I returned to the living room with Angelo. His father told him it was time for a nap and Angelo did not object when he was tucked into bed. Jacob and I talked for about 15 minutes more, then I told him I was leaving. As I had my hand on the doorknob, he said, "Could I ask you one more question?"

"If it is a short one," I smiled.

"Have you decided who will get custody?"

"Mr. Norcross, I still have a great deal more work to do in the evaluation."

"Well, just give me a hint about who you are leaning towards."

"You're anxious about this, aren't you?"

"I'm scared sick of losing Angelo."

"Angelo needs both parents in his life, now and for years to come. To lose either of you would be a tragedy. Believe me, I am aware of that. Going through an evaluation like this is really hard on parents. I'm sorry it has to be that way."

"Well, I guess we'll just have to see how things go."

"I'll call you next week. Goodbye for now."

Home Visit—Jennifer Norcross

Jennifer had moved into a beautiful building that used to be an old mansion before it was converted into apartments. The interior was lovely. Her living room was flooded with light from a large window composed of numerous squares of glass edged with lead. A grey-and-mauve toned Chinese carpet covered the floor. I wondered where she got the money for such an expensive carpet.

She offered me Jasmine tea and we spoke for a few minutes about the building and its history. Then I asked where Lisa and Angelo were. They were in the bedroom, playing. They were inseparable companions, she added, and always played beautifully together. I requested that they come out so that I could be with the whole family together.

Lisa had one of those elfin faces that you see in fairytale books, smooth and pale with large sober eyes. She seemed shy and sat next to her mother in silence. Angelo carried one of his famous trucks in his hand. He sat in the middle of the room on the floor and rolled it back and forth without sound effects.

I had the feeling that a "family discussion" would fall a little flat at this point, so I decided to launch into a structured project. "I would like to get to know you as a family," I began, "so I thought we could begin with an activity. I have brought some paper and crayons. Let's find a place where you can all draw together. Oh, here on the table is fine. I want you to draw a picture together. It doesn't matter what it is. Just let your imagination guide you. All three of you should participate."

Jennifer and Lisa went immediately to the table. Angelo did not look up from his truck until his mother called him over. The mother picked up some crayons and began drawing a large house, quite competently. Lisa added an apple tree on the far side of the yard. Angelo watched them. "You draw, too," Lisa said to him. He stirred the crayons around a bit, then selected a brown one. He scribbled something on the roof of the house.

"What are you doing, Angelo?" the mother said, placing her hand on his to quiet his motion for a moment.

"Coloring," he said.

"I tell you what. You color over there on that side of the paper and I'll do the roof, okay?"

"Okay," he said without seeming to care.

"Very nice," she commented to him as he scribbled something that resembled a tornado turned on its side.

The completed picture was interesting. A nicely sketched three-story house with eaves and awnings adorned the center of the page. Lisa's apple tree stood on the right with a little chubby girl who looked about three years old standing under it. Angelo's brown whatever-it-was swirled on the other side of paper.

Lisa seemed more relaxed now and was gazing at me with interest as her mother and I talked about the household routine. I directed questions at the girl whenever possible. "Do you have chores around the house? What do you like to do with your mom and Angelo to have fun? Do you have any friends in the neighborhood?" She answered in a quiet voice that was unusually low and melodious for a child. I directed questions at Angelo also, but he had no patience for hanging around the three of us. He played with his trucks and finally withdrew to his bedroom for at least 20 minutes.

I had arranged to have lunch at Jennifer's house. The table was already set with midnight blue stoneware plates and a vase of flowers. Jennifer asked me to sit down and offered me wine. I chose cranberry juice instead, but told her to feel free to have wine if she liked. She said she would have juice also. I could smell something good but could not identify what it was. She came out of the kitchen with a hot casserole of salmon and hard-boiled eggs in a white cream sauce, covered with breadcrumbs. A basket of homemade zucchini bread was also presented. "This is wonderful," I smiled. "Do you always cook like this?"

"Yes, I love to cook," she said. "In the marriage I did all the cooking. This is something I worry about if Jacob got custody of Angelo. He can barely fry an egg. I'm afraid that the child would eat most of his meals at Burger King or eat spaghetti at

Grandma's every night. He also has no concept of nutrition. We had arguments often over sugar in the kid's diets. He loads them up with sugar. Did you notice that at his house?"

"Well, you two have different lifestyles, I did notice that," I hedged.

Lisa liked the lunch, but Angelo only picked at his.

"What food do you like your mom to cook for you, Angelo?" I asked. "Is your mom a good cook?" But the question didn't work this time, and he just gave me sullen stare.

"Answer the lady, Angelo," the mother interjected.

"I don't like food," he pouted.

"Get down from the table, then," she said without anger. He did so and disappeared into his room again.

"Is Angelo feeling bad about something?" I asked Jennifer. "Is he tired, perhaps?"

"No. Meals are a problem for him. He rarely eats at the table; then he asks for a snack a half hour later. His dad gives him so much junk that his eating habits are ruined."

After lunch I said that I wanted to spend time with both Lisa and Angelo together. Then I wanted to see them separately. They shared a bedroom. It was attractively decorated with yellow curtains and matching spreads on the twin beds. A bookshelf with at least 50 children's books and a set of children's encyclopedias stood on one wall. "Does anyone read you these books?" I asked the children.

"Mom does sometimes," Lisa said. "I read to Angelo sometimes, too, but I can't read the hard books."

"When your dad lived here, did he ever read you books?"

"No. He just watched T.V." I told the children that I would like to watch them play a game. Did they have one that they like to play together? Yes, Candyland. The game was easily found on the neat shelf of toys in the closet. As they moved their little pieces through the molasses swamps and gumdrop fields, I watched their interaction. For the most part, they played independently of each other and seldom talked. Each took a card and moved the piece. Sometimes Angelo would move his too far and Lisa would move it back to the right place in an irritated manner. Angelo became upset because he was "stuck" on a square and had to wait until he drew a certain color card. Lisa looked smug as she raced by him. He then picked up the pile of cards and tried to shuffle them like playing cards, spilling them all over in the process. Lisa slapped his hand in frustration, then started to cry. "He always ruins everything," she said through her tears. Angelo did not cry but watched her in fascination.

I said, "It looks like we have had enough of this game. Let's pack it up. Lisa, could you and I spend a little time together? Angelo, later I would like to play with you for a while. Right now, why don't you pick a few toys and take them into the living room where your mom is?"

After the individual sessions with each child, I wanted to spend the last 20 minutes with the mother alone. Angelo had fallen asleep and Lisa went over to play with a friend in the neighborhood. "We didn't talk as much about Lisa as we could have," I began. "Although custody is not in question with her, she is part of Angelo's family. Tell me, what kind of relationship does she have with her biological father?" Jennifer related that Lisa never knew her natural father because she was only a year old when the marriage broke up. He came around to the maternal grandmother's house where Jennifer and Lisa were living, but everyone made it clear that he was not welcome and he dropped out of the picture. It is just as well, Jennifer said, because he was something of a low-life. I asked her what she meant. She was referring to the fact that he was a truck driver, smoked dope, and came from a lower-class background.

What about Lisa's relationship with Jacob? What was it like during the marriage and what will it be in the future? Jennifer said that Lisa and Jacob got along well. Just like a child, he loved games and would play with her endlessly. Other than that, he really didn't contribute too much to her life. Jennifer said that Jacob has complained to her because Lisa is not coming over to his house often anymore. She thinks that more visits are unrealistic. Lisa never regarded him as her real father, and except for seeing each other occasionally, she doesn't feel that Jacob and Lisa should artificially maintain that relationship.

Departing, I looked around for the children. Then I remembered that Jacob had fallen asleep. "Lisa probably went to a friend's house," Jennifer said. "I'll say goodbye for you." But as I opened the car door, I saw Lisa sitting on the driveway by my front tire.

"Lisa, I'm glad to see you. I wanted to say goodbye." She leaped up, gave me a quick, hard hug, then bounded away on her skinny white legs.

5

Working with Children

No custody study can succeed unless it competently assesses the needs and feelings of the children in question. If the evaluator cannot penetrate these issues, who can? Parents are generally caught up in their own emotions and may have distorted perceptions of the situation; they often confuse their own desires with those of their children. Attorneys are pledged to represent the interests of their adult clients. Judges occasionally speak in person with older children, but this is the exception rather than the rule. The only person, other than the evaluator, who works with children directly is the Guardian ad Litum (or the attorney for the child). They may be appointed by the court or may be hired by parents to represent the children's interests. They often undertake extensive investigation into the custody issues. Unfortunately, these professionals are seldom used in custody cases.

Every mental health professional doing custody work has (or should have had) previous experience working with children in a therapeutic setting. How children progress through successive stages of development, how they exhibit various forms of distress or "disturbance," how they express feelings in words and behavior, and how they may be reached in communication are issues already understood by the practitioner. But custody evaluations require a slight shift in orientation. We use the same skills but apply them differently. In an evaluation, our main task is information gathering and assessment, not therapeutic intervention. We do not have the luxury of weeks and months of sessions with a youngster. Every moment must be used to the best advantage, yet must be as constructive as possible for the young interviewee. The evaluator knows in advance that these will be the most tender and the most difficult hours of the whole study.

We usually do not interview children first but wait until the evaluation is underway. We want to have established some background on the case so that key questions are already forming in our minds. Generally, these questions will fall into the following categories:

(1) How well is this child functioning physically, intellectually, and emotionally?
  Specific issues that will be explored in this category are:
  (a) Do the child's motor skill abilities and physical development seem normal for his or her age?
  (b) How is the child progressing cognitively and intellectually, based on our observation and on reports from parents, teachers, and others?
  (c) Does the child's emotional maturity seem appropriate for his or her age? Is there evidence of emotional problems? How is he or she functioning socially, both at home and at school?
(2) What kind of relationship does the child have with each parent?
  (a) What degree of attachment does the child evidence toward each parent? For example, in what ways and to what degree does he or she view each parent as a source of security? Does he or she prefer to spend more time with one parent than the other? What kinds of activities does the child like to do with each? With whom does he or she tend to identify?
  (b) How well does the child communicate and share feelings with each parent? For example, how free and spontaneous does he or she seem with each? To whom does the youngster go for advice or to discuss an important issue?

    (c) How well does the child respond to each parent's methods of setting limits? For example, is the child too complying or overly rebellious with either parent?

(3) What does the child feel about the custody issues?

    (a) What are the child's stated feelings? For example, does he or she seem eager to state a preference about where he or she would like to live? Does he or she close down or display anxiety when the custody issue is broached?

    (b) What are the child's unspoken feelings? Is the youngster communicating something through behavior, fantasy play, stories, or other means that suggests certain feelings and attachments? Are these consistent with his or her stated preferences on the matter? Or is he or she saying one thing but feeling another?

In addition to these basic questions, the evaluator will have a list (mental or written) of issues to investigate that are specific to the case at hand. For example, the mother has said, concerning her twelve-year-old daughter, "The only reason Judith wants to live with her father is because she feels sorry for him being all alone. I don't think that's a good reason." Hearing this, the evaluator will make a special effort to understand how Judith views her father, whether she feels she should be taking care of him, how much emotional support she actually receives from him, and so forth. How does this compare with the relationship Judith has with her mother?

Some information on these concerns has been gathered by observing parent-child interactions. But much of it can only be obtained by working individually with children. The following techniques, categorized in terms of children's age groups, represent only a few of the hundreds that might be employed. Some are variations on methods used by child therapists. Experienced evaluators will find themselves spontaneously creating new techniques to deal with situations that arise. This is desirable. We should remain fluid in the use of such tools, sometimes allowing intuition to guide our choices. Remember that the final outcome will never be determined by one method or one piece of information alone.

Infants to 36 Months

Anyone who has attempted to "interview" a child under 30 months old probably did not repeat the experience. It is obvious that other methods of information gathering must be employed here. Direct observation of the child, assessment of parent-child interaction, and interviews with persons who know the child will form the basis of our work with youngsters under three years old. Understanding the history of the child's relationship with each parent will provide additional clues about the child's attachments and life experience.

If necessary, evaluators should shape up their knowledge of what developmental tasks are expected of children between the ages of birth and three years old. Table 5.1 abstracted from several sources, provides a quick reference.

If we find that a child in question is seriously lagging behind in a developmental area, we will want to speak with the child's physician. If there is no physician, we may recommend to the family that a "developmental screening" be conducted to detect possible problems. These evaluations are usually available at modest cost through county or state agencies. Because of time limitations, the evaluation often must be completed before this screening is completed. But such a process will benefit the child, regardless of the outcome of custody. It is also important to note whether both parents seem equally concerned and responsive about the suggestion of a screening. It may reflect something about their willingness to obtain assistance for the child when needed.

Three to Five Years Old

Some of the following techniques may be used with verbally advanced children under three years old. The evaluator may intitiate the first one and see if the child is able to play along. If not, the activity can easily be abandoned. These approaches are designed to tap into the fantasy life of the youngster. By doing so we bring out feelings, experiences, and imaginings that may relate directly to the family issues at hand.

(1) "Mommy's house, Daddy's house" (or adjust for situation involved, e.g., "Grandma's house, Mommy's house") This may be played with stuffed animals, dolls, puppets, or small figures belonging to the child. If no such objects are available, the evaluator can draw two houses on two sheets of paper; simple figures of dogs, kittens, or teddy bears are then drawn and cut out to represent actors. Children of this age group tend to relate more freely to animal characters than to human ones. Animals are also less threatening because they are one step removed from the intense human situation of the child. Have the child select figures to represent members of his or her family. Place the two houses in separate locations. Introduce the activity by saying something like, "Now this little bear (the one representing the child) has a family just like yours. The daddy lives over here in this house and the momma lives over in that house. Sometimes the little bear stays with momma (put bear there) and sometimes she stays with daddy (put bear there). Where should we put the little bear?" Now watch what the child does and follow her lead, encouraging her to develop the action. For example:

> Child: Put the bear with momma.
>
> Evaluator: Okay. You be the little bear. I'll be the momma. Hello Little Bear!
>
> Child: Hello momma! (child makes two bears kiss)
>
> Evaluator: What happens next?
>
> Child: The momma bear says, Let's play.
>
> Evaluator: Let's play.

Table 5.1
Quick Reference Developmental Chart
(infants to 36 months)

Age (months)	Gross Motor Skills	Play Skills	Language Development	Self Awareness and Interpersonal Development
1-2	Grasps object voluntarily (not reflexively) when placed in hand	Holds rattle briefly	Makes small noises in throat	Looks at face of adult Follows moving person visually Smiles responsively
3-4	Lifts head high while on stomach Rolls from stomach to back	Reaches for and grasps toy held near hand Shows interest in play-things	Laughs Vocalizes spontaneously to self and toys	Initiates contact by smiling or vocalizing
5-6	Rolls from back to side Head doesn't lag when pulled up into sitting position	Shows displeasure at loss of toy	Turns towards voice of another	Tends not to smile at strange faces Notices and plays with own foot
7-10	With support, can sit with trunk erect; Crawls on belly; Stands with help	Transfers object from hand to hand Plays with two toys simultaneously	Vocalizes "da" "ba" "ha" Vocalizes "mama" "dada"	Plays pat-a-cake, so-big with others Pushes away intruding hand

Age (months)				
11-13	Walks a few steps without help; Crawls up stairs; Seats self on floor	Favors "putting in and taking out" game	"Can say two different words besides "mama" or "dada"	Enjoys rolling a ball to another; Feeds self with fingers
15-18	Walks alone; Can climb into adult chair	Throws a ball; Looks at picture books; Explores drawers and cabinets	Can say four to six different words; Can name one or two common objects	Hugs and gives kiss; Can identify at least a few parts of body (eye, nose, mouth)
18-24	Runs well; Walks up and down stairs; Kicks ball on request	Can turn pages of a book one at a time; Pushes small cars about; Can build a tower of several small blocks	Combines two or three words spontaneously; Has vocabulary of 20-25 words; Begins to use own name	Recognizes own reflection in mirror; Imitates parents in domestic activities (sweeping floor, etc.)
24-30	Stands on one foot; Walks on tip toes; Walks backwards a few steps	Holds crayon with fingers; Helps put toys away	Uses personal pronouns "I" "me" "you"; Gives first and last name; Says simple sentences, i.e. "Daddy come here"	Relates to animals and toys in personal, nurturing manner, i.e. takes care of a teddy bear; Plays games with others such as tag
30-36	Pedals tricycle; Feeds self with little spilling; Puts on shoes; Buttons and unbuttons	Can kick a small ball without falling; Can copy a cross and circle from page	Uses plurals; Can name objects in picture	Can say what sex he or she is; Understands taking turns; Separates from parents easily

Child: O.K., let's play cooking. (Bears make motions together) Let's take a bath. Let's go to bed.

Evaluator: Where does the little bear sleep?

Child: Next to the momma.

(the evaluator asks other questions that illuminate activities or patterns in the family, for example, "Does the little bear ever get a spanking? What does the momma bear fix the little bear to eat? How does the little bear like the brother bear? And so forth.)

Evaluator: Now the little bear has been at the momma's for a while. It's time to go be with the daddy.

Child: O.K. Bye, Mom. I'm going to daddy's.

Evaluator: What does the momma bear feel about that?

Child: (as momma bear) Don't go, Baby Bear! I'll be sad. I want you to stay and play with me.

Evaluator: What does the little bear want to do?

Child: I want to go see my daddy. I'll be back. Don't cry, mom.

This short exchange suggests several things to the evaluator that can be explored further: (a) the girl placed herself in her mother's house first; does this reflect a primary desire to be with her mother? Compare with other data; (b) the girl seems to perceive a close relationship between mother and daughter, one that also has a quality of being "playmates" to it. Do mother and daughter sleep together each night? Or is this just a wish of the child's? These factors could point to an overly symbiotic (dependent and enmeshed) relationship between the two; check this against other information; (c) the girl perceives her mother as dependent on her and feels the need to "take care of" her mother emotionally by comforting her. How much does this reflect the interaction between the two of them? (d) despite the pressure from her mother to stay, the girl insists on going to her dad's house. Some children would have refused to send the little bear to dad's under these circumstances. This suggests a desire to spend time with her father; what is their relationship like?

In using this technique, the child should be encouraged to play the roles of both child and parent. The best situation is one in which the child begins doing this on his or her own spontaneously. The evaluator must participate enough to keep the action going, but should not get too involved in one of the parts. Otherwise the direction of the action may be overly influenced. Open-ended questions such as "What does the daddy say now?" "What does the little kitten want to do?" "Why is the dog sad?" produce the best results. In every "play," make sure that the child figure goes from one house to the other. The reactions that arise around this could be informative. One little boy, for example, buried his toy deep under the blankets when told that it was time for the dog to leave his paternal grandmother's house and go on a two-week vacation with his mother. (The boy lived with his grandmother.) When the evaluator, as the "mother" dog, knocked on the door, the boy said, "All the babies are sleeping now. Come back later." Asked why the little dog didn't want to let his mother in, the boy said, "He's afraid his mother will never bring him back, ever again." The mother had once taken the child for three months without returning him to his grandmother's home. His statements reflected his fear of being away from his grandmother for a prolonged period of time.

If, in the course of the game, the child becomes disruptive, refuses to continue, or otherwise displays anxiety, this suggests serious distress around the separation or custody issues. The evaluator may try to inquire about this, saying, "Looks like you and the bear are feeling (mad, sad, scared, and so on) about this," and see what the child says. Then it is best to switch to a more neutral activity for a while.

(2) "Calling Mom, Calling Dad" This is particularly effective if one parent has been absent or is living a long distance away. Children between four and five years old seem to do best with it. The evaluator and child each have a telephone, which may be blocks of

wood folded pieces of paper, or toy phones. The evaluator says, "Let's call your dad" (or one of the parents). The evaluator begins by playing the role of the parent, but steps out of that as soon as possible, becoming the evaluator again and encouraging the child to talk. The child is also encouraged to play the role of the parent. For example:

Evaluator: Ring! Hello, this is your dad speaking.

   Child: Hello dad.

Evaluator: Go ahead and talk. What would you like to say to your dad?

   Child: When are you coming to see me?

Evaluator: Ah, you want him to visit you. What else do you want to say to him?

   Child: If you don't come and see me, I'll kick you in the leg.

Evaluator: You're mad at your dad for not being here.

   Child: Yeah.

Evaluator: Anything else you want to tell him?

   Child: No.

Evaluator: Then why don't we switch it around? You be the dad on the telephone. Ring!

   Child: Hello, this is dad.

Evaluator: Hi, this is Stephen.

   Child: (as father) I'm way far away in Georgia.

Evaluator: What are you doing there, dad? (testing his understanding of the situation)

   Child: I'm mad at you and mom and I'm staying here for 20 years.

Evaluator: Why are you mad at me?

   Child: You're a bad boy and you hit the baby twice and you made your mother cry.

The evaluator suspects from this exchange that the child feels abandoned by the father, resulting in sad and angry feelings. He also blames himself for the father's departure. What kind of contact has the father maintained with the boy since the separation? What sorts of messages is the mother giving the child about the separation? Has anyone in the family noticed that the boy is carrying this burden? These are questions that the evaluator will want to address.

Reading the above "telephone conversation," one feels the tug to help the boy deal with his pain in some way. In a counseling session, the therapist would have steered the development in a different direction at several points during the conversation. The evaluator, however, must stay focused on finding out how the child is feeling. Sometimes a little therapeutic work can be accomplished without sacrificing the discovery process, but often the evaluator must leave the child's room with an aching sense of not being able to help. Yet the mere fact that someone in authority has noticed these problems can benefit the child. In the final feedback session, both parents can be told about the child's feelings and entreated to deal with them. Counseling can be strongly recommended in the written report.

(3) "If you could change yourself into an animal, what animal would you be? Why?" This brief game can yield useful information under some circumstances. Children enjoy it, and it provides relief from the heavier emotional atmosphere of the previous techniques. The animals children choose reflect aspects of their desires. Do they wish to be fierce, powerful animals that could roar and scare people? This may result from a feeling of helplessness and inconsequentiality. Perhaps it suggests that the child would like to have other family members pay more attention to his or her angry feelings. Does the youngster wish to be a little mouse that can hide in a corner, perhaps to avoid being hurt? A beautiful pet that everyone will care for? Sometimes, of course, the evaluator does not obtain too much from this, except perhaps a smile, as when one five-year-old announced that he would like to be "a goldfish because no one ever tries to make them eat avocados!"

(4) "If you could have three wishes, what would they be?" A child's wishes often reflect a lot about his or her needs and desires. Matters relating to the divorce and custody are often included in these. For older children, the wishes provide a good opening to discuss their feelings.

(5) "Island Game" This is the famous island game that exists in many forms and nearly always provides insights about children's attachments. I am not fond of the brief version in which the adults simply asks the child, "If you could choose one person to live on an island with you, who would that be?" Particularly for children under six, this hypothetical question may not be clear. The evaluator will obtain better results by developing a story and drawing little pictures (inept as they may be!) to illustrate. The pictures tend to captivate children's attention and enable them to connect better on the words. Here is one version that can be used: "Once upon a time there was a little girl who lived on an island all alone in the middle of a big ocean. (Draw water and simple island with figure on it). The girl had everything she needed—food, water, a bed, toys, and everything. (Draw little items on island). But she was missing something. She was very lonely because no one lived there with her. One day a magical fairy flew to the island (draw) and said, 'I know you would like to live with somebody here. You can choose one person and I will bring that person to you.' Who does the little girl choose?" Let her answer. If she says, "My parents," which often happens, say, "We can only have one person come. Who will that be?" After the child answers, draw a second figure on island. "Now the little girl felt much better. One day the magical fairy came back and said, "I can bring one more person to live with you. Who should that be?" Child answers. (Draw new figure). Finally the fairy came back and said, "Now you can have whomever you want come to live with you. You tell me who they are, and I'll bring them." (Child names them. Encourage her to name as many as she wants and write them down in the order she says them). "Well, the fairy looked down at the island and said, 'You know what, I think

that island is becoming too crowded. I'm going to take you all back to the land where you live.' And Poof, everyone went back and lived happily ever after." This format gives children the satisfaction of hearing a completed story and distracts them from the anxiety of having to "choose" key others to live with them. Sometimes a youngster will repeatedly refuse to select someone or may insist on choosing both parents. If the child seems distressed, do not press the issue, but let both parents come to the island, or whatever the child prefers. Then finish the story.

Five to Eight Years Old

As children get older, fewer techniques are needed for communicating with them. Kids of this age love talking about their activities, friends, and favorite possessions. Nearly anything in the room can be used as an opening conversation-piece.Unless the child hates school, he or she will be pleased to show the evaluator papers and drawings done in class. All drawings should be noted carefully for clues to the child's feelings. It is also important to understand who is typically involved in the child's school activities and who assists with homework. Parental involvement with the child can also be discerned by asking questions about items in the child's room: "Those are great science books. Who bought them for you? Does someone help you read them?" "Who made all those nice labels for your rock collection?" "Wow, what nice wallpaper and bedspreads. Whose idea was it to fix up your room like this?"

Because friendships are one of the most exciting things happening in the lives of these children, time should always be devoted to this subject. But the evaluator's real purpose is to learn about the child's social development and the family's role in this. A child may be asked to name his or her best friends, for example. If he or she cannot name any, something is probably wrong, and the matter should be investigated later. Does one or both parents keep the youngster isolated? Regarding the child's friends, the evaluator will want to inquire where they live, whether they ever spend the night, whether the child visits their houses, which adults do the transporting, and so forth. A parent's ability to foster the child's peer relationship is an important factor when considering custody.

In addition to purposeful conversation, the following techniques may assist information gathering.

(1) The three wishes technique may be used well with this age group. The evaluator can make special use of it to lead into more detailed discussions of the child's desires and feelings. For example, and eight-year-old boy says, "My first wish would be to have a go-cart." We ask him all about what type of go-cart he would prefer and what he would do with it. In the course of the conversation it comes to light that the boy would like to have his father build it with him and spend weekends at the go-cart track a few miles away. The boy and father often went there together before the separation, we learn, but with the father's new girlfriend and all, there isn't much time for that sort of thing anymore. Thus the wish for a go-cart really translates into a desire for the father to spend more time with him. This will be valuable information, both for the evaluation and for sharing with the father later.

(2) In whom can you confide? By this age, children already have a sense of how successfully they can confide in each parent and be understood. But they are unable or unwilling to verbalilze this. By setting up a few hypothetical situations and asking the child what he or she would do, this information can be elicited. Here is an example of how the situation might develop:

Evaluator: This is a game for your imagination. I want to see what you would do if you found yourself with a certain problem. I know that you don't really have this problem; we're just pretending. Suppose that a friend of yours stole some candy and gum from the 7-11. This friend came over to your house and said, "Lindsey, I stole this stuff from the store, but now I'm afraid I'll get caught. If my parents find out, they'll punish me good. So I'm going to hide it under your bed. Now, don't you dare tell anyone, or I won't be your friend anymore. I'll come back in a few days and eat some of it. If you want to eat some, you can take a little." Then the friend goes home. Now you really have a problem. What would you do?

The evaluator notes whether the child decides to confide in anyone. If not, there is probably a lack of trust and communication in the family. The child should be asked, "Are you sure there is no one you would talk to about this? Otherwise you are stuck with the problem all by yourself." Sometimes a child will pick a teacher or neighbor. Usually, though, the child says that she would tell a parent, or "parents." This should be explored. For instance:

Child: I'd tell my parents.

Evaluator: Who would you tell first, your mother or father?

Child: I think my father.

Evaluator: Why would he be the one you would go to?

Child: He always listens. He understands things that you say to him.

Evaluator: If you told you mother about it, what would she say?

Child: I don't know. She might think I stole the candy. Well, maybe not. But she gets mad for no reason a lot of times.

Evaluator: If neither of your parents were around, who would you talk to about this?

Child: I guess my older brother. I'm tired of this game.

Evaluator: So am I. Let's look at your horse collection.

The evaluator should have a repertoire of two or three hypothetical situations that involve problems a child of this age might have and that would require the advice of an adult to solve. Because the child will be seen twice, once at each home, the procedure may be repeated with different "problems." Here are some other possible topics that could be used:

> Your friend loaned you his Sony Walkman and said to take good care of it. But now you can't find it. You are afraid you have lost it. You want to tell someone about this problem. Whom would that be?

> Your teacher seems to have a grudge against you. Nothing you do in class is right. You feel like talking to someone about that. Whom would that be?

> Last night you had a terrible nightmare. You can't seem to get it out of your mind. It scares you just to think about it. If you tell someone about the dream, you might feel better. Whom would you tell?

> You heard something in school that made you feel embarrassed. It had to do with sex. You aren't even sure if it is true. You think you should talk to an adult about it. Whom would you talk to?

(3) Best and worst features of living at each parent's. This is a casual introduction to the topic of the child's living arrangements. One says, "I understand that you have been spending time at your dad's house and at your mom's house. Let me get this right—you stay at your dad's from Monday to Friday, then you go to your mom's on Saturday and Sunday. Is that right? Tell me, what is the best thing about being at your dad's, and what is the best thing about being at your mom's? Let's start with your dad. (discussion of this ensues). Now let's switch it. What is the worst thing about being at your dad's and the worst thing about being at your mom's? Revealing and surprising details of everyday living often emerge from this line of questioning.

(4) Draw your family. Therapists and evaluators have long depended on this technique for understanding children's feelings about the family and their place in it. The child is given a full-sized piece of paper, pencils, and crayons, and asked to draw a picture of

his or her family. If the child asks, "Who should be in it?" "What should the family be doing?" or similar questions, the evaluator says, "Draw it any way that you like." Watch the child as he or she draws. Whom does he or she draw first? Is there hesitation or a sense of anxiety about this task? How are family members positioned in relationship to each other? In particular, where has the child placed him—or herself in relation to the others? One seven-year-old, for example, drew her mother and younger brother close together, holding hands, her father some distance away in a detached position off the ground, and herself standing at the far side of the picture with her dog. This strongly suggested that she felt alone and separate in the family, with only her pet to comfort her. Subsequent work with her confirmed this. One nine-year-old boy drew himself, two siblings, and mother, plus his live-in aunt and her two children cramped into a canoe. Crocodiles threatened them in the surrounding water. This undoubtedly conveyed the experience of his current living situation, which entailed serious economic threats and unhappy family members (the aunt had just separated from her husband).

After the child has completed the drawing, ask him or her to name the family members and tell what they are doing. The evaluator should write the names of each person on the drawing because it is easy to forget who is who. If the child appears to be interested in this activity, he or she can be encouraged to add dialogue to the picture, cartoon style. "What is the dad saying?" "What words should be put in this person's mouth?" The people are deliberately not identified as "you" or "your dad" to allow more freedom of fantasy for the child.

(5) Complete the sentences. This is also a popular tool that exists in many forms. Copyrighted versions called "Sentence Completion Tests" are available from The Psychological Corporation, New York. Evaluators may originate their own wording in order to address issues of importance. The beginning of sentences are presented, and the child is asked to complete them. For this age group, doing the exercise orally seems to work best. A light atmosphere

should be maintained. "Just say anything that comes into your mind," we tell the child." This isn't a test of any kind, it's just for fun." When the child responds to the first item, we compliment him or her and encourage him or her to do others. If the child balks at an item or "can't think of anything," we note this, for it probably has evoked anxiety. All of the child's responses are written down for future reference. Some sample items are as follows:

   (1) My favorite animal is . . .
   (2) I have fun when . . .
   (3) Sometimes I feel worried about . . .
   (4) My friends . . .
   (5) When I stay with my father (or other litigant) . . .
   (6) My favorite food is . . .
   (7) When I grow up . . .
   (8) When I stay with my mother (or other litigant) . . .
   (9) School . . .
  (10) I feel sad when . . .
  (11) My brother (sister) . . .
  (12) Sometimes I wish that . . .
  (13) The nicest person in the world is . . .
  (14) When I was younger . . .
  (15) The worst thing about divorce is . . .
  (16) If I took a trip I would like to . . .
  (17) I feel really mad when . . .
  (18) I wish that my mother . . .
  (19) I wish that my father . . .

The evaluator could add other sentences pertaining to specific features of the case. For example, "My mother's boyfriend . . . ," "The new house my father has . . . ," "My aunt . . ."

Ten Years Old and Older

Youngsters in this age group are well aware of the custody dispute and role of the evaluator in the situation. It is, therefore usually a good idea to begin right at the heart of things rather than to attempt to make chitchat. I usually say something like, "You probably know why I wanted to talk to you alone. My job is to understand what kind of living arrangement might work out best for you. Your feelings are very important to me." For some children, these opening statements are enough to uncap a rush of words and feelings. They may tell the evaluator instantly where they want to live and why. A discussion can then ensue about why the child feels as he or she does. "What do you think would be better about living most of the time at your dad's?" "Suppose you didn't end up living there. What would it be like to live with your mom most of the time?" "Are there some disadvantages to living with (parent of choice)?" "How do you think your mom would feel if your dad got custody of you? (then switch question around)" "What is the worst thing that could happen in this custody situation?" Questions such as these help open up the young person's thoughts about the subject.

The child may not respond to the opening invitation. In that case, the speech can continue along the lines of: "Even though I am interested in your feelings, nobody wants you to choose between your parents. You should have contact with both of them, no matter how this custody situation turns out. What are your thoughts on this?" A similar approach may be used with more mature children in the previous age group.

Even if a youngster seems clear about his or her preferences, using indirect techniques to probe feelings is recommended. Among these are the following:

(1) Draw your family. This approach, discussed earlier, is useful for the older age groups. Imaginative youngsters can be asked to add dialogue to the figures, cartoon style.

(2) Complete the sentence. For this age group, the sentences can be typed on a piece of paper and the answers written by the children. They should be assured that this is not a test of any kind and that they should feel free to jot down anything that comes into their minds. The evaluator is encouraged to make up a list that seems useful. The following sentences provide ideas.

 (1) The thing I like to do best in my free time is . . .
 (2) I wish . . .
 (3) Sometimes I feel worried about . . .
 (4) My friends . . .
 (5) When I am with my father (or appropriate litigant) . . .
 (6) Someday, when I am older, . . .
 (7) When I am with my mother (or other litigant) . . .
 (8) School . . .
 (9) It makes me sad . . .
(10) My brother (sister) . . .
(11) The person I can always count on . . .
(12) I am happiest when . . .
(13) The worst thing about divorce is . . .
(14) If I took a trip, I would like to . . .
(15) It makes me mad when . . .
(16) I wish that my mother . . .
(17) I wish that my father . . .

(3) The worst and best thing about being with each parent. This is excellent for older children. It gives them a chance to air gripes, perhaps ones they have never put into words before, about both parents. It also makes them evaluate positive experiences about each household. Enough time should be devoted to this exercise to allow ample discussion.

Confidentiality

One of the most difficult issues an evaluator faces when working with children is that of confidentiality. Ordinarily, a therapist encourages a child to share his or her most intimate feelings, assuring him or her that this will be kept secret unless the child gives permission to share it. But in an evaluation, this pledge obviously cannot be made. Parents, attorneys, judges, and the public at large will learn of a child's feeling if the matter is aired in court. Even if the case settles before court, parents must be informed of basic realities concerning the child's feelings. There is no easy solution to this problem. The best an evaluator can do is to try to protect the child's feelings as much as possible while functioning as a conveyor of information. The following suggestions may help achieve this.

First, when working with children, comment periodically, "You know, I think it would help if your parents understood how you felt about that. Would it be all right if I let them know in some way?" and see how the child responds. Frequently, children are relieved that someone will help them express these things. If a child says, "No, I want it kept a secret." The evaluator should explore this and ask what he or she is afraid would happen if his or her parents know about these feelings. This will be valuable information for the evaluation. If the child is insistent, even after discussion, the evaluator can respond, "I promise you that I will do my best to protect your feelings about this. I won't tell anyone the exact words you said to me. But I have to give people a general idea of how you feel, or no one will be able to solve this family problem we have." Nearly all children will find this acceptable.

Second, in writing the report, children should not be quoted unless the evaluator has a special purpose in mind. The example report in Chapter 2 did include a somewhat unique quote from a child. It was designed to add warmth to the document and to convey the genuineness of his feelings. Generally, though, it is much better to make general statements about the child's feelings. Phrases that can be used include:

Molly appears to feel that (e.g., her mother is more understanding of her than her father).

Johnathan conveyed by his words and behavior that (e.g., he felt more secure around his father).

Andrew's communications suggested that . . .

In this way, the evaluator takes responsibility for interpreting the child's input. It takes the heat off the child. Imagine a parent reading in a report, "Molly told the evaluator that her father is a cold, unsympathetic person who has no understanding of her feelings. In contrast, she said that she felt very close to her mother and wanted to live with her most of the time." One can see the consequences for a child of being quoted in this manner.

Third, when speaking with parents in the final feedback session, they should be helped to understand their children's feelings. This should be done without quoting the children. But the evaluator can become the children's spokeperson and get the message across with diplomacy. For example, "Mr. Parent, I was glad to talk to Molly at length because I believe I now understand some of her feelings about the situation. There appears to be some lack of communication between you and Molly. She loves you, but she wishes that you would tune into her feelings more and understand her a little more. Have you had difficulty communicating with her?" In this way the message is conveyed in a manner that will not hurt parent-child relationships.

If we bring our "therapist-self" to each session with a child, we can do our work as evaluators yet create a constructive atmosphere. The opportunity to discuss feelings, reveal fears, and share hopes can be therapeutic in itself for the young interviewee if we handle the situation with sensitivity. For some children, it will be the only time that someone really listens to them. The irony of this was underscored by a 12-year-old girl who said at the end of the evaluation, "Why is it that before the divorce, no one gave a hang about what I had to say? Now suddenly you grown-ups act like my feelings are the most important thing in the whole wide world!"

CONTINUING CASE STUDY
Norcross vs. Norcross

Individual Interview—Lisa

Lisa was still a little upset from the gameboard incident as we began the session. I hoped she would talk about it.

"It's tough to have a little brother sometimes," I said. She looked at me somewhat wonderingly, as though she weren't accustomed to anyone saying this. "I know," she answered. "He gets into all my things. He broke my umbrella last week. He caught it on a bush and all the covering tore off the metal toothpick things."

"Did you tell your mother?"

"Yes."

"What happened?"

"Nothing. She had to go shopping."

"Sounds like you feel nobody took your side."

"Nobody ever does. Sometimes Jacob did, but only sometimes."

"Can I ask you a question about Jacob?"

"Sure."

"I understand that you haven't been over there in several weeks. I'm wondering how you feel about that."

She looked down at her skirt and didn't say anything for a few moments. Then she shrugged and said, "I don't know."

"You aren't sure how you feel?" I asked, giving it one more try. I could see by her face that the topic bothered her.

"Well, he and mom are getting divorced. He's not my real dad. My mom and I have talked about how he isn't my real dad. But I feel sort of sad anyhow. You know what I mean?" She regarded me a little warily, as though I might object to what she said.

"Of course you feel sad. You have been living with him a long time. He was part of your family and now he's gone."

At this, Lisa made a choking sound and began to shake all over with quiet sobs. I lay my arm across her back as she buried her face in the pillow. In a few minutes she stopped. I said, "You know, it's all right to cry when we feel sad. Especially when we have lost someone we love."

"Can I see Jacob again?" she asked.

"I would like for that to happen. Would it be okay with you if I talk to your mother and Jacob about this and see what we can work out?"

"Will my mom be mad?"

"Why would she be mad?"

"She doesn't like him anymore."

"But you do."

"Yes."

"I'll do my best to help her understand. I can't promise that things will be perfect, but maybe they can get better."

We talked about other topics—school, her friends, her grandparents. She used to miss her (maternal) grandmother a great deal; she still remembers that. But after a time, she got used to being with her mother and Jacob. She has only seen her grandmother three times in the last five years. Her grandmother and mom had some sort of fight; she wasn't sure what it was all about. What about her other grandparents, the Norcrosses? Her face lit up at the mention of them. "They love me just like they were my real grandma and grandpa," she said, "and I love them." Then her eyes filled up with tears again and she asked me if she would see them anymore, now that everyone was getting a divorce. I replied that I would talk to the grown-ups about it and see what we could do.

By the end of the session, the girl was practically sitting in my lap. I hoped that she would not ask me if she would see me again because I knew that the probability was slim of that happening. But she didn't ask. By now she was probably wary of asking that question. In one way or another she had already lost most of the important people of her life. She said nothing as I left her room.

Individual Interview—Angelo

I was beginning to see that Angelo didn't connect with people as easily as he connected with things. His eyes were always darting here and there, and his hands were in perpetual motion. During the session at his father's house, I managed to get his attention with a game I made up about trucks in a garage. There is a momma truck, a daddy truck, a sister truck, and a boy truck. I let Angelo pick the boy truck so that he would identify with it more. They used to all live in the same garage. But one day they decided that they couldn't all live there anymore. So the mother and sister went to live in a new garage (I put them a few feet away). The boy truck sometimes stayed with the dad and sometimes stayed with the mom. Well, where should the boy stay now? He can go anywhere he wants. Without hesitation Angelo placed the truck with the father. "Why does the truck like to be there?" I asked.

"He has fun. He likes it there."

"What does he like about it?"

"He just likes it." I had done it again—asked a question too advanced for him. So we played trucks for a while. I encouraged the truck to spend time at both garages and have fun with the other trucks. But Angelo was not willing to leave the truck with mother and sister for too long.

If he could change himself into an animal, what would that be? A monkey, like he saw in the zoo with his dad. I had to smile at that. He reminded me of a cute little monkey, with those large eyes and restless movements. Does he ever dream? Yes, but he couldn't remember any. Does he ever have scary dreams? Yes, a robot comes after him, "real slow, with scary eyes that keep staring and staring."

At his mother's house I tried the island story. He picked his father to come live with him on the island. When the good fairy said he could have another person join the two of them, he picked his mother. When the fairy said he could have a third person come, he said that he didn't want any more people.

"How about Lisa?" I asked.

"Naw, she can stay home and play with her friends."

We did a last game concerning a family of monkeys (for Angelo's sake) who go on a trip together. Seeing no stuffed animals with which to play, I drew pitiful representations on a sheet of paper. But Angelo was fascinated nonetheless. First they have to go searching for food. They decide to split up and go different ways; then they will all meet back at the tree in the evening. Mother and sister monkey go one way and father goes the other way. Who does the boy monkey want to go with? With mom and sister. Which group finds the food and brings it back? Mom's group. Good. Now it's night time. They can't find a cave that is big enough to sleep in, but they find two little caves. "Some of us will have to sleep in this cave, and some of us will have to sleep in that cave. Where should everyone sleep?" I let Angelo place monkeys in the caves. He puts himself and Dad in one and Lisa and Mom in the other.

Angelo was looking tired. I had timed the home visits so that I was at each parent's house from 11:00 to 2:00 or 2:30. It was probably time for his nap. I said, "Are you getting tired, Angelo?" He nodded wearily and walked over to the bed to lie down. Before I could say goodbye, he was snoring as loudly as a man.

6

Interviewing Collaterals

Collateral literally means "situated at the side" or "accompanying, attendant, auxiliary." For our purposes, it refers to those individuals other than the parties centrally involved in the custody dispute. Generally this will be friends of the family, teachers, physicians, and others who may have significant information to share. Judges and attorney seem to appreciate it when the evaluator has interviewed several collaterals as part of the study. This method parallels their own discovery process in which evidence is gathered from many sources before a conclusion is drawn. Evaluators realize privately that some of this collateral work is wasted time because the sources have nothing of importance to say. But because one can never predict ahead of time where the nuggets will be found, each area must be searched conscientiously.

The most productive interviews will almost always be with professionals who have had contact with the children. Primary among these are counselors, teachers, daycare personnel, physicians, and possibly dentists. Next in line are lay persons who have had a neutral relationship to the child, such as babysitters, sports coaches, and scout leaders. Never fail to interview babysitters if possible. They witness the home situation as it really is and see parents and kids at their best and worst. Unlike friends of the family, they usually do not have strong desires to defend either parent, so the truth will be closer to the surface. The following conversation between evaluator and babysitter is not atypical.

Evaluator: Tell me a little about Jamie's father. You babysit for him, I understand.

Babysitter: Oh, he's a really a nice guy.

Evaluator: What do you find nice about him?

Babysitter: He always pays me a little extra. He really appreciates my babysitting for him so often.

Evaluator: Are there things that you sometimes don't like about him?

Babysitter: No. Well, yes. It makes me a little mad when he says he'll be back at 7:00 and doesn't show up until 11:30 at night. The kids keep asking where he is; then they finally fall asleep. My mom doesn't like it either because I get home late.

Evaluator: How often does this happen?

Babysitter: He only did it two nights this week. Last week was worse.

At the lowest rung of importance are the parents' friends and members of the extended family, such as aunts and cousins. I know many evaluators who never contact collaterals in this category. But they may be losing something by adopting this policy. Judiciously interviewing a friend or family member, no matter how biased the informant is, can produce important pieces of information at the most unexpected times. The key is to avoid letting them seize control of the conversation and thereby waste your time. Concrete suggestions on how to structure these interviews to best advantage will be discussed presently.

A second benefit of interviewing friends and relatives is that parents feel more satisfied with the evaluation process when they know you have talked to their "champions." "Talk to my best friend, Sharon Jones. She can tell you all about me," is a common sentiment among litigants. To the uninitiated, it is difficult to believe that an evaluator could ever understand the situation through direct experience of the family alone. Surely, they think, the only way to know a person is to ask all of their friends and relatives about them.

Here are some guidelines for interviewing various types of collaterals. It will be seen that the questions address the basic areas of inquiry discussed previously. That is, they are concerned with a further probing of the physical, emotional, and social factors that determine a child's quality of life. By this point in the evaluation, we will already know a great deal about the family. We will have obtained a sense of each parent's desires and concerns regarding custody; the children will have been seen in interaction with both parents; both home environments will have been evaluated; the children will each have been interviewed or observed privately and information about their needs and feelings will have been obtained. The collateral interviews are designed to check facts, fill in missing information, and provide new facets to our understanding.

Obviously, much of the wording in the following discussion reflects my own style and may not be appropriate for anyone else. My intention is not to discourage other approaches, but to provide specific ideas for structuring the conversation. Interviewees tend to open up or close down depending on how we phrase things. The beginning moments of an interview are particularly important. Everyone benefits from the information gained in a smooth, productive conversation.

Interviewing Teachers

It is advisable to send teachers a letter several days before the scheduled conversation because it prepares them for your call and enables them to review their files. The letter may look something like this:

Dear Teacher,
I have been asked to carry out a custody evaluation concerning a student of yours, Bobby Martin. I am a neutral evaluator whose job

it is to understand this family and recommend a good plan for the children's living arrangements. I would appreciate talking to you about Bobby's academic progress, his emotional adjustment to school, his relationship with the other children, and a few other topics.

Bobby's parents know that I will be talking to you. If you have any questions regarding this permission, please contact them. I will be phoning you within the next few days. Thank you for your assistance.

Sincerely,
Custody evaluator

Some evaluators send a checklist for the teacher to fill out, rating the student on academic achievement (excellent to poor), social adjustment, appearance, and so forth. I feel that it is too much to expect a busy professional to fill out one more form and return it. People are also reluctant to put things down in writing. Often these forms are never returned. Telephoning seems preferable, particularly because more specific, personalized information can be gathered.

If there is no time for preliminary letters, then the evaluator must call "cold." The best time to call is about 20 minutes before classes start in the morning, or right after school ends in the afternoon. The receptionist who answers the phone at the school can tell you what these times are. It is also a good idea to introduce yourself to the receptionist when you call so that you will be put through more easily when you call back. Once the teacher is on the phone, it is important to identify yourself and your agency, if applicable, and add that you are a neutral evaluator, and so on, as you would have done in an introductory letter. Unless the teacher clearly understands that you are representing the best interests of the child, he or she will be guarded or uncooperative. If teachers seem reluctant to talk because of confidentiality issues, encourage them to call the parents and tell them that you will phone again in a day or two. To make doubly sure that things go through, it is best to call the parent and ask him or her to call the teacher directly.

Teachers are often worried that you will ask them who they believe should have custody of the child. So I usually say in the beginning, "I certainly am not going to ask you who you think should have custody of Heather, because no one knows the answer to that question at this point. I'm interested in your perspective of Heather as a student and as a little girl. For example, how do you feel she is doing academically right now?" This is a great opening question for teachers because it puts them on comfortable, familiar ground: academic performance. After they answer this, the following questions will generally prove helpful:

—How does the child relate to other students in the class? Do you feel that her social development is appropriate for her age? Have you observed any problems in this area? (If that doesn't elicit satisfactory information, a more specific approach could be used, such as, "Would you describe the child as isolated? outgoing? aggressive?")

—Have there been any behavior problems with this child? Could you describe them?

—In terms of physical appearance, how does this child compare with other students? Do you have an impression of his being well cared for, or do you sense negligence there? Is he usually dressed appropriately for weather conditions?

—How has this child's attendance been? (if there have been many absences, ask the reasons). Is the child brought to school on time each day?

—Have you had conferences with the mother? the father? Has the mother (father) been involved in other ways, such as participating in school activities?

—What is your impression of the mother's (father's) concern for the child? Has he or she seemed willing to help the child at home or to follow your suggestions?

—Has the child ever indicated anything to you that expressed strong feelings about the divorce or custody situation?

Once these basic areas are covered, you may have some specific questions to ask that will throw light on allegations raised in the study. For example, the father has alleged that the mother often forgets to give the child lunch money. You can ask the teacher whether or not there have been problems with the child not having lunch money. The mother alleged that the child never seems to do her homework when she is staying with the father. You can ask the teacher if there have been problems with homework, and whether there had been any pattern to this problem.

Interviewing Daycare Personnel

Key questions for daycare teachers and directors will be:

—When was the child first enrolled in the daycare center?

—Who enrolled him or her?

—How do you feel the child has adjusted to the daycare setting?

—How does the child relate to the other children? To the teachers? (Would you rate him or her as isolated, social, aggressive, and so on?)

—In terms of developmental skills, how is the child progressing? Do you feel that his or her skills are up to par for that age? (if not, get specifics).

—Who generally brings the child each morning? At what time? Who picks him or her up each day? At what time?

—Have there ever been problems with a parent being late picking up the child? Please describe these.

—In your opinion, does the (person who brings the child) provide him or her with appropriate clothes and supplies? (If not, get details on this).

—I would appreciate hearing some of your observations on the mother-child (father-child) relationship. Does the mother seem warm and caring when she drops off or picks up the child? Does the child run to her when she arrives? What does her mood usually seem to be like? (other specific questions may be helpful here.)

Questions targeting allegations can be asked now. The father alleges that the mother brings the child to daycare even when the child is sick. This can be checked out. The mother claims that the father is erratic about the child's schedule so that the youngster often misses activities and is out of step with the other children. The daycare teacher can comment on this.

Interviewing Physicians

Nearly all physicians will require having a written release in hand before they will talk to you. Even a handwritten document such as: "I give Dr. Takahashi permission to talk to Dianne Skafte, custody evaluator, and to release any information or records about my child and myself," signed by the parent and dated, will suffice. A formally drawn up release with the evaluator's letterhead on the paper is better. In many states, only the custodial parent can give permission for releasing information about the child. So if temporary custody had been granted to a parent, make sure that this parent signs the letter that should be sent to the doctor and that the letter expresses these thoughts:

Dear Dr. Takahashi:

I have been asked to carry out a custody evaluation concerning the children Michael Johnson and Sarah Johnson. I am a neutral evaluator whose job it is to recommend a good plan for these children. I understand that (name patient) is a patient of yours (or has been a patient of yours). It would be helpful to me to talk to you briefly about (his or her) medical history. Enclosed is a release signed by (the patient or child's parent). I will be calling your office in a few days to arrange a convenient time to speak with you.

Thank you very much for your assistance.

Sincerely,
Custody evaluator

Sometimes, the doctor turns the task over to his or her receptionist, who consults the records in response to your questions. This is less helpful, but important information can still be obtained. The questions will vary depending on whose physician it is and what the allegations are in the case. The most intensive questions will be asked of the children's doctor.

—When did the child first start coming to you?

—Do you have a record of who first brought him or her?

—How many times has the child been brought in? Generally speaking, is there a pattern to these visits? Once a month? Once every six months? Who has typically brought the child into your office for treatment?

—What is your assessment of this child's general level of health? What, if any, are his or her major problems? Do you feel that there are any external factors contributing to these problems, such as stress, health habits of the parents, environmental conditions?

—In your contacts with the father (mother), has he or she seemed responsive to the child's health needs? Has he or she followed through with suggestions you have made or instructions you have given?

—Do you have any impressions or opinions of the adults' parenting behavior that you feel would be helpful to this evaluation?

Specific questions can be added that highlight allegations. For instance, the aunt related that the mother didn't take the child to the doctor until the child's ear infection was far advanced. The doctor could be asked to refer to an ear infection around the date in question and to give an opinion on how far advanced the ailment was. It may also be helpful to ask the doctor what he or she told the mother about the seriousness of the illness. This information should be compared with the mother's account of the episode.

Interviewing Psychologists, Psychiatrists, or Other Therapists

Whether or not to interview the family's therapists is a delicate question. As mental health professionals know, the therapeutic relationship depends on maintaining trust with the patient or client. Any involvement in a custody dispute, no matter how well intentioned, could inject unpredictable and negative elements into the process. As evaluators, we wish to protect this island of emotional safety for parents and children. Such islands are especially necessary during the traumatic times of custody conflict. For this reason, some evaluators refuse to interview therapists who are currently involved with the family.

If we do choose to speak with a therapist, it will be necessary to have a written release signed by the parent or parents. Most important, we should be clear about our purpose for making the call. It is inappropriate to ask the therapist questions that we are supposed to be answering ourselves in the course of the evaluation. For example, we should not probe a therapist about the parent's real feelings toward the children; we should not inquire whether a patient really wants custody or is just trying to manipulate the other parent; we should not expect a child psychologist to tell us who the better parent is; we should never ask whether an individual is "capable" of assuming the full-time duties of single parenthood. These are matters of judgment that require a broad basis of investigation before they can be understood. Furthermore, such questions place the therapist in a difficult position. Suppose, for example, the psychologist privately feels that his or her patient probably cannot handle full-time parenthood. What is the therapist going to say to the evaluator? If he or she tells the truth, the relationship with his or her patient may be permanently ruined. But if he or she "distorts" the truth, the child's future may be jeopardized.

Interviews with therapists should focus primarily on the therapy process in a general way. When did the parent first come to you for therapy? In your opinion, is he or she making satisfactory progress? What do you see as his or her psychological strengths? (It is best not to ask about weaknesses). Is there a way of projecting how long the parent might be in therapy? The following questions might be asked of the child's therapist: When did the child first start coming to therapy? Do you remember which parent initiated this? Has the child been brought on a regular basis? In your opinion, what are the major issues this child is working on? Are you satisfied with the progress the child is making? Is there a way of projecting how long the therapy process will need to continue?

We should always let the therapist know that we understand their need to protect the relationship with their client. We should implicitly give them permission to say nothing if they think it would be better. In that way, we will have done our duty in making the contact but will not have jeopardized a greater future good for a minor present gain.

Interviewing Lay Persons

Neutral lay persons such as babysitters, music lesson teachers, coaches, scout leaders, and others in similar positions are often valuable sources of information. Included in this category is the parent's employer or supervisor, who sometimes should be interviewed. These conversations can usually be kept short because the persons involved have only seen the child or parent under specific circumstances. For example, the evaluator might want to ask the sports coach how the child seems to be doing in sports, how the child relates to the rest of the team, and which parent appears to be the most involved in these activities (who brings the child to practice, who attends the games, and who has contributed time to the team.)

Occasionally we have concerns about how well a parent can function vocationally. The parent tells us that her current job is wonderful, that she is doing great, and that she will be staying there for a long time. In this case, it would be essential to talk to the supervisor or employer briefly, asking questions such as, "How is Ms. Peterson performing at her job? Have there been any problems? How does she get along with the other employees? What is her current salary? A surprising number of parents give the evaluator the wrong information about salary. In your opinion, does she have a future with your company?" Sometimes a parent's greatest strength is their ability to maintain a good job and do well in the work setting. Therefore, an employer may be contacted just to demonstrate this fact.

Babysitters need more extensive interviewing. The following lines of questioning to babysitters will usually open up areas of importance:

—When did you first start babysitting for (the child)?

—Who arranged for you to come?

—How often do you babysit? (Get a detailed picture of the pattern of babysitting, including what time the babysitter typically comes and leaves, whether the babysitter ever stays all night, whether the babysitter works on weekends, and so on.)

—Tell me a little about (the child). What kind of kid is she or he? What do you enjoy most about him or her? Do you ever have any problems with him or her? (If there is more than one child, ask how the children get along and try to get details about their interaction).

—Tell me a little about the parent. What things do you like about him or her? Are there some things you think could be improved? (Get concrete observations from the babysitter).

A considerable portion of the interview will be spent addressing issues that may concern you or that have been brought up in allegations. If the mother's nutrition habits are in question, for example, you will want to ask the babysitter what kind of food the mother usually has in the house and what the child usually eats. If it has been alleged that the father loses his temper easily, you will want to ask the babysitter about the father's moods and his behavior toward the children, particularly under stress.

Interviewing Friends and Family Members

Generally friends and family of the litigant already know that you will be calling. Often they have rehearsed their information with the litigant beforehand. This will usually be a rehash of all the allegations. Sometimes friends or family members are so caught up in the dispute that their intensity gushes out in great fountains of words that cannot be quelled. For all of these reasons, interviewing these collaterals can be annoying for the evaluator.

Such problems can never be avoided completely but can be mitigated by having a clear plan for the interview. Basically, the evaluator should take control of the conversation from the beginning and avoid open-ended dialogue. This structuring can be accomplished in many ways. Here is a sample model of one approach:

"Hello, Ms. Day, I am Dianne Skafte, a custody evaluator (mention agency if applicable). I am doing a study on the Richards family, trying to understand what would be best for the children, Robin and Peter. Ms. Richards gave me your name. Perhaps she mentioned that I might be calling. (interviewee answers).

"I won't keep you on the phone too long (hint, hint) but I would like to ask you a few questions. Is this a convenient time to talk?" (answer) "Let me say before we begin that I am a neutral party in this. I am not on anyone's side. My only concern is for the children. I am most interested in your direct observations of the family. I won't be asking you who should get custody because no one knows that yet. Do you understand what I mean?" (hope that the answer is yes). "There is something else that is important. The information you tell me could conceivably end up in the final report or could be repeated in court. I will not quote you unless I absolutely have to, but you need to know that what you tell me cannot remain confidential. So keep that in mind as we talk, okay?

"Let me ask you first, do you know the entire Richards family or just Ms. Richard?" (It is important to determine from the outset the extent and nature of the collateral's contacts with the family members. Some collaterals have never met the mother but will tell you at length how awful that mother is. Some collaterals, particularly those whose connection is through the job setting, have never seen either parent with the children but will attest to what a fabulous father we have here.)

"How long have you known Ms. Richards? Are you a neighbor? Do you know her through work? Have you had opportunities to be in her home and see her with the children? Approximately how often?" (If the collateral has not been in the home or has not seen the parent with the children, you may want to ask a few questions about the parent's character, for example, "What are some of the traits that you admire most about this person? How is this person regarded at work? Is she considered reliable and conscientious? Are there traits about this person that you think could be improved?" But if the collateral does frequent the home, observations about the parent's behavior and the parent-child interaction should be obtained. Sometimes, such a collateral can be useful in clarifying past history also. Lead-in questions such as the following could be used.

"Let's look at the strengths and weaknesses—we all have them—of Ms. Richards as a mother for a moment. What things do you think she does especially well as a parent?" (If the collateral makes general statements such as "She really loves the children," or "She is really patient," try to pin them down about what they have observed that makes them say that.) "How could Ms. Richards improve as a mother, do you think?" (Again, get reports of concrete observations. If the collateral says, "I think she could stay home with the children a little more," say, "Have there been times when you thought she wasn't staying home enough? Tell me about a few of them.")

"It sounds as though you know both parents. Tell me, how are they different from each other in their parenting styles? Do they discipline the same way, for example?" (This is a good opening question because it is framed in nonjudgmental terms. Usually the collateral will begin talking about the parents. The evaluator can then stop the speaker and ask for concrete observations.)

"You knew both of the parents around the time when Peter was born. How did each of them react to having a new baby? Did they both share in the tasks of changing diapers and feeding Jason? Do you remember any problems that either of them had?"

After the more global questions are asked, you may decide that this collateral can provide information to shed light on a specific concern or allegation. It can be broached in this way: "In the course of this study, a concern has been raised that I wanted to mention to you." (Never share the source of the allegation). "The issue involves Ms. Richard's boyfriend, Allen. There is a question of whether Allen spanks Peter too harshly sometimes. Do you have any knowledge of this?" (If yes, get details. In any case, probe the collateral's observations about boyfriend and child together.)

After the questions you prepared have been answered, collaterals may be aching to tell you about their feelings concerning the custody dispute, about their own children, about their sister's divorce, about how they would love to do your kind of work, and so forth. Sometimes I let the collateral talk for a short time out of sympathy for their need to express their feelings. But the interview must be ended within a reasonably short time after the main line of questioning is completed, or the evaluator will begin to feel fatigued and valuable time will be wasted. An effective way to end the conversation is to cut them off gently with, "Excuse me, Ms. Collateral, but I must go now. I want to thank you for your kind help. If I find that I have other questions, I'll call you again. Is that all right?" ("Oh yes," they usually say.) Then you can say, "Thank you," and hang up before they take the next breath.

Naturally, careful notes should be kept on collateral interviews. Quote marks should be placed around significant statements of informants, making it clear that they phrased information in that particular way. This might prove to be helpful later when you have to testify on the witness stand about what a particular collateral said.

At the end of the evaluation, the evaluator looks at the bundle of notes on collateral interviews and cannot help but feel that some of it was wasted effort. True, some interviews failed to provide information directly useful, but the total result of the effort is never wasted. Talking to all of those people who have known the family provides a gestalt, a filling in of the puzzle pieces, that cannot be obtained any other way. Sometimes the information one absorbs is more subtle than specific facts and dates. Did you notice that most of the father's friends and relatives seemed warm, fair-minded, and genuinely concerned for the child? And the mother's people seemed more quick to blame and less concerned for the children? Does this reflect something about each parent? Or, it became clear that information gathered from a mother's collaterals fit well with her account of the situation. But information from the father's collaterals was full of contradictions and was at odds with his own reporting. Observations such as these will contribute significantly to the way the scales tip in the final stage of the evaluation.

CONTINUING CASE STUDY
Norcross vs. Norcross

I assembled a list of collaterals I wanted to interview. They included Angelo's babysitter, Angelo's daycare teacher, Lisa's teacher, each parent's employer, and the names that Jennifer and Jacob had provided me. Because there have been no allegations regarding health or health care, I skipped the doctors. Here are summaries of what I found out from each collateral.

Ms. Cindy Fields, babysitter. Cindy babysits Angelo and Lisa at the mother's house. She is the 15-year-old daughter of a resident in the apartment building. Her parents are usually home so that if an emergency arises, she can depend on them. Typically, the babysitter watches Lisa and Angelo two evenings during the week while Jennifer attends classes. I asked what time the mother gets home from classes on week nights. Between 9:00 and 10:30, depending on whether she goes out with friends or not. How do Lisa and Angelo usually get along with each other when they are together, I asked? Sometimes okay, but sometimes not so good, she told me. She feels that most of the fights are Lisa's fault. Lisa seems to blow up at the smallest thing and then starts to cry. It has gotten worse in the last few weeks.

Ms. Marjorie Howard, Lisa's third grade teacher. Because school recently ended, Ms. Howard knew Lisa well, having been with her a full academic year. She characterized Lisa as a "semi-loner," meaning that the girl had a few friends but was not too social and spent a lot of time by herself. She did good academic work. About three months ago, after her parents separated, Lisa began having difficulty paying attention in class. She would stare out of the window, and one day she failed to respond even after the teacher called her name twice. Ms. Howard hoped that this would improve as time went on, but in fact it seemed to get worse, particularly toward the end of school. Has the teacher had any contact with either parent? Yes, they both attended the parent-teacher conferences. Mr. Norcross gave a special presentation to the class one day about planting a garden, which the children loved. Other than that, neither of them have made special appointments or been particularly active in the programs. Often, when parents are getting divorced, either a mother or father will come in to tell the teacher about it so that everyone can watch for problems. But neither of the Norcrosses did this.

Ms. Betty Burkenstein, Angelo's preschool teacher. Ms. Burkenstein was one of those cheerful, enthusiastic teachers that everyone wishes they had had as kids. "Angelo! Oh yes, what a doll! I could talk about him all day," she responded when I introduced myself and told her what I wanted. Angelo has been attending that preschool for a year. The teacher said that he is a little dynamo, a race car whose engine is always revved up. He wants to experience everything at once. Sometimes this gets him in trouble with the other children because he impulsively grabs their toys, then is genuinely shocked when they cry or get angry. I asked her whether the school did any reading-readiness or prekindergarten academic work. Yes. But Angelo did not quite seem ready for that yet. Whereas some children showed interest in learning letters, he did not. He was still in the down-on-the-floor-pushing-trucks-around stage. Yes, I certainly agreed with that. Had she had much contact with either parent? She has spoken with the mother several times, never for long. The mother seems like a lovely woman. She is interesting to talk to. The teacher has had several long conversations with the father. He seems to be crazy about the boy, and that is always a joy to see. One afternoon the father brought his guitar to the school and sang Italian and American songs to the children for over an hour. They flocked around him like a pied piper. Ms. Burkenstein said that she was sorry to hear about the separation. Who told her about it, I asked? The father came in one day and explained the circumstances to her. But fortunately, she had not seen any adverse effects in Angelo so far.

Dr. Michael Davis, Jennifer's employer. Jennifer works half-time as a receptionist and secretary at the University Admissions Office. She has held that job for nine months. Dr. Davis complimented Jennifer highly on her work. He said that she is a real asset to the office because of her personable manner and intelligence. She organizes her work well. He feels that eventually they will lose her because she is too capable for that position in the long run. But he hopes she will stay for as long as possible.

Mr. Bob Sutton, the father's employer. Mr. Sutton owns the nursery and landscaping company where Jacob had worked

for six years. He related that Jacob was one of his best employees, perhaps the best. He was reliable, could be trusted
with any job, and had an artistic eye. He thinks Jacob should
have his own business someday. Mr. Sutton also knows Jacob's father. He commented that the Norcrosses ("How did
Italians get a name like that?" he interjected) are a good, solid
family and are well-respected in the community.

Ms. Doris Byrd (name provided by the mother). Ms. Byrd attends the university and has known Jennifer for a year and a
half. She thinks Jennifer is one of the most remarkable people she has ever met. She is creative and interested in the
world. Her insight into people is extraordinary. Has Ms. Byrd
spent much time with Jennifer and the children? No, not really. She has seen the children a few times at Jennifer's
house, but has not talked to them. Has she met Jacob? Only a
few times. But Jennifer has told her all about him. Ms. Byrd
thinks it was inevitable that they separated. Somebody like
Jacob simply can't expect to hold a woman like Jennifer. Not
for long, anyway.

Ms. Rebecca Florien (name provided by the mother). Ms.
Florien knew both Jennifer and Jacob during the marriage.
She also has known both children for about three years so I
planned to spend slightly more time talking to her. How were
Jennifer and Jacob different from each other in their parenting styles, I asked? Jacob had a more emotional approach
and Jennifer had a more intellectual approach, she said. Jennifer read a lot of books and took psychology courses. Sometimes her friends would come to her and ask advice about
their children. Jacob wasn't much of a reader, but he had a lot
of natural love of kids in him. His parents are wonderful; you
couldn't help but adore them. They were always hugging each
other and everyone else within fifty feet of them. What kind of
relationship did Lisa have with Jacob? According to Ms. Florien, Lisa was always hanging on Jacob. He treated her like
his own daughter, and that meant getting gruff with her sometimes. But they seemed to have a good relationship. Appar-

ently Jennifer is dating a graduate student in psychology now. Does Ms. Florien know him, I asked? Yes, his name is David. He is a dream of a guy. Unlike most graduate students, he has a lot of money and buys Jennifer expensive gifts. For example, he bought her an unbelievably beautiful Chinese carpet. Does their relationship seem serious, as far as Ms. Florien can tell? Yes. He proposed to her. Jennifer said she may accept, but that she wants to wait until this custody thing is settled before she makes any decisions.

Mr. Bart Ribe (name provided by the mother). Mr. Ribe has been a friend of Jennifer's for two years. He has not met the children. Mr. Ribe said that I shouldn't be deceived by what Jacob might tell me about himself. He is not what he pretends to be. I asked him to explain this further. Mr. Ribe remembers Jacob from high school as a "disgusting fag who would get puking drunk and cry like a girl." I asked him whether he meant that Mr. Norcross was a homosexual. Mr. Ribe hesitated for a moment and said, "You draw your own conclusions." I said that I needed to understand each parent as thoroughly as possible, because the child's future depended on it. I asked again for clarification. The collateral said, "I wouldn't know him that well to say for sure. But you can look at those big pretty eyes and sissy face and take a pretty good guess." I asked Mr. Ribe whether there was anything else that he wanted to say about either parent. Yes, he wanted to say that Jennifer is probably "the most together woman you will ever meet" and that I would be crazy not to give the kid to her.

Ms. Harriet Jankowski (name provided by the father). Ms. Jankowski is a woman in her mid fifties who has known Jacob since he was a child. She also knew Jennifer and the children during the marriage. I told her that I was interested in understanding Jacob and Jennifer as parents. Any observation she had about their relationship with the children would be valuable. She began by saying that she was sure that they both loved the children. (I felt good about this because it suggested that Ms. Jankowski might be fairly neutral in her accounting). She said that the mother always kept a good house and was a good cook. The kids looked better than most because she dressed them in nice clothes. The father gave them a lot, too. He always had time to listen to them; at night sometimes he would sing songs for them; he was usually the one who gave them their baths and tucked them in bed, although the mother did this sometimes. Angelo especially was wild about his dad; he would shriek with joy everytime his dad came in the door. I asked her whether she had any concerns about the way either parent handled the kids. That is, how could each parent improve, in her opinion. She said that Angelo was sort of at a loss now that Jennifer was gone. He was so heartbroken at first that he cried like a baby for weeks. His sister and mother had to take care of him because he couldn't even make himself a hamburger. Ms. Jankowski worried that it wasn't good for the kids to see him so upset and helpless. If he had custody, well, it wouldn't be easy for him at first to do everything for Jacob that Jennifer did.

I asked whether she ever observed him to drink more than he should. She was silent for a moment, then said, "I have to say yes. I love Jacob, understand. But I'll be right up front because of those kids. When he was in high school he did his share of drinking and shooting up the town. Well, not really shooting it up, that's just an expression. I mean racing that Thunderbird up and down the streets with his pals. He settled down a lot after he started working. In the last few years, no, I don't think he drinks more than any other working man. He likes his wine with supper, and I've seen him drink a beer or two with my husband at my house. Nobody in his family drinks very much. I don't know if those things are carried in family lines or not, but sometimes they seem to be." I asked her if she had any concerns about Jennifer as a mother. "That's harder to put into words," she answered slowly. "But yes, I do. She can be warm one minute and cold as ice the next. One evening she was at our house having dinner with Jacob and his brother and wife. She was being charming as only Jennifer can be, with that pretty laugh that makes everyone happy. Then her eyes got sort of glazed and she just sort of stared straight ahead. Pretty soon, without a word, she got up and went home. I asked her the next day if someone had made her mad or something. But no, she said she just got tired. I've seen her do this at least a half dozen times. But it's when she does it with the children that bothers me. I sometimes think she looks right through them as if they weren't there. Just a few months ago, before the breakup, I was at her house. Lisa and Angelo were having one of their spats. Angelo picked up a glass of milk and dumped it in Lisa's lap. Lisa slapped him, right across the face. I jumped up, about to run over there. But Jennifer just stared at them like she was watching a T.V. program. I don't know if she really saw what happened or not. But she was looking right at them. Jacob used to holler at her for this all the time, but she would just tell him he knew nothing about children or anything else." I thanked her for her time and cooperation. Just before we hung up, she said. "Could I put my two cents in about this custody thing?" Sure, I said. "I think that kids should always go with their mother, even if the mother isn't the greatest. Jacob is one of the best fathers I've ever seen, but a little kid like Angelo belongs with his mom." I thanked her again and dialed the next name on the list.

Ms. Constance Norcross (name provided by the father). Ms. Norcross is Jacob's sister-in-law. I had told him that I preferred references that were not family members, but I decided to call the collateral anyway. Ms. Norcross had babysat with Lisa and Angelo a lot since Angelo was born. The children loved Ms. Norcross's two sons, who were about the same ages as Lisa and Angelo. In Ms. Norcross's opinion, Jennifer was always eager to have the kids stay with someone else. Jennifer was one who loved to go, go, go, Ms. Norcross said. Ms. Norcross volunteered that she always believed Jennifer was having affairs during the marriage, and she once saw her downtown with a tall blond fellow while she was supposed to be in class at the university. But Ms. Norcross never said a word to Jacob because she didn't want to cause trouble. The sister-in-law said that she was secretly relieved when the marriage ended because they could not relate well to Jennifer. Jennifer always seemed to feel that she was better than they were. She even said, right in front of everyone, that Jacob's father was "in the last analysis, ignorant of everything that is important." The family was hurt by this but never said anything. I asked Ms. Norcross how well she thought Jacob would do if he were saddled with the full responsibility of a son to rear. She said that whatever he lacked, the family could fill in, for they were all helpful to each other.

Mr. John Fernando (name provided by the father). Mr. Fernando apparently is a man of few words, and I had difficulty getting many out of him. How long have you known Mr. Norcross, I asked. "Quite a long time, " he would answer. And what is your relationship to him? Are you friends, do you work with him, or what? "We've known each other for quite a long time."

Have you had the opportunity to see Mr. Norcross with the children? "Yes." Could you share with me your impressions of Mr. Norcross as a father? For example, how did he handle the children? "He's a good father." Is there any specific thing that you have observed that makes you say he is a good father? "Just in general, he is good." I see. Do you know Jennifer Norcross at all? "Saw her a few times." Well I want to thank you for your help. Is there anything else you would like to say about this matter? "No, I guess not." Well, goodbye then.

7

Pulling it All Together: The Final Judgment

Now that the long information-gathering phase of the evaluation is largely completed, we must step back from the hundreds of facts, fictions, and impressions that surround us and try to achieve a more holistic view of the family. Otherwise, all that follows will have a scattered quality.

If our custody case involves a divorcing family—and most do—the picture looks something like this. We have a mother and father who used to live under the same roof, rear their children together, and think of themselves as one unit. As soon as they separated their household, their entire orientation changed. They now find it almost impossible to associate with each other or to see themselves as having goals in common. They are struggling to redefine the family in a way that makes sense to them. But they are failing in this. Unlike most divorcing couples who are able to work out a plan for their children on their own, our couple falls into the minority who must let the court make these decisions for them. Their primary need now is for resolution, peace, and getting on with the business of rearing their children. We suspect that this will not come easily for them.

Under these unfavorable circumstances, what is the best situation for the children? We must automatically reject the easy answers if we are to serve the family well. Parents, well-meaning friends, and untutored professionals proffer many of these. A favorite proposal is to divide up the children, Solomon-style. This may entail giving half of the children to each parent (if we are lucky enough to be working with even-numbered progeny), or it may involve giving each parent a strict 50 percent of the children's time. These remedies have a certain common-sense appeal. The flaw is that they are designed to satisfy the needs of the parents, not the children. As will be discussed later, there are many reasons why such arrangements could be negative for youngsters.

At the other extreme of the easy-solution continuum is the attempt to "simplify" things by squeezing one parent out of the picture. In court decisions, this often takes the form of ordering skimpy visitation for a mother or father (usually the latter). But the pressure to eliminate a parent almost always comes from adults, not children. Clinical experience and a growing body of research suggests that children can deal with two households and can handle their new, complex family relationships (e.g., stepmother's father or stepsister's mother) quite well. They are skillful at incorporating both families into their framework and finding satisfaction there. But this healing and integrating instinct often encounters relentless opposition from adults who are trapped in their decayed patterns and wish to perpetuate the misery for all family members.

Any of the above arrangements—splitting up siblings, recommending a 50 percent-50 percent time-sharing plan, or greatly reducing the input of one parent—could be appropriate under certain circumstances. Sometimes siblings have different needs and preferences. Sometimes a child would do better moving back and forth between households than losing the balance of what each parent can offer. Sometimes a parent is so psychologically toxic or generates so much turmoil in the family that the child must be protected from too much exposure. The point is that we cannot fall back on patent solutions in custody work. Nor can we be led astray trying to pacify the desires of the adults involved.

The best plan for the child, therefore, will be the one that maximizes his or her chances for full development of the "self" in the new family structure. For our purposes (and for court testimony later on), we identify three primary aspects of the self: the physical, the emotional/social, and the intellectual. The child must be nurtured in all three areas to thrive successfully in the world. Each parent can contribute differently to this process. What living situation and time-sharing plan will provide the child with the best from each parent? The answer to this one question constitutes the "best interests of the child."

Our task now becomes a little clearer. We will tackle the heap of data that we have collected and evaluate it in terms of the following questions: (1) What are this child's physical, emotional/social, and intellectual needs at present? (2) What will these needs be in the future? (3) How well and in what ways are litigant A and litigant B able to meet these needs? When we say "litigant," we actually mean the total environment that the litigant offers. For example, if a father has a warm, supportive network of friends and extended family members, this is something that the father offers. One's physical, emotional, and intellectual environments should be regarded as extensions of oneself. During the transition of divorce, though, we must sometimes look beyond the present circumstances and endeavor to understand what a parent's typical patterns are. For instance, a mother may be living in a house with four roommates who create disruption and who are not considerate of the child. Is this typical of the environment she chooses? Or has she usually gravitated toward peaceful home settings but was forced by economics to live here temporarily? Understanding the parent's past history will help us evaluate these factors.

Let us take each question by turn and see how it serves as a data-organizing tool.

What are this child's present physical, emotional/social, and intellectual needs? Clearly, the age of the child will be a determinant here. Our knowledge of developmental psychology guides our understanding of what children need at various ages of maturation. From birth to about 18 months, the child's physical experiences will have enormous impact on the development of the "self." Consistent, attentive physical care is a primary need. The child will begin to learn that the world is a trustworthy place if he or she is fed when hungry, picked up when troubled, cuddled often, and provided frequent contact with those people he or she has come to depend upon. How well can each parent give the child this? Look at the evidence. Perhaps one parent has been performing this task well already and the other has only been on the sidelines. The amount of time spent with the child is not the only factor to consider. Sometimes the "caretaking" parent has been carrying most of the child-care load with frustration and resentment, and the other has interacted eagerly with the child whenever the chance arose. Observations of parent-child interaction will provide essential information here,and collateral interviews will probably have provided other clues. Often, both parents will be working. In this case, neither of them will be with the child for most of the day. In addition to their attitudes and behavior regarding the youngster, we want to look at their ability to set up good child-care arrangements. Who seems to have the best record and the best instincts in this respect? We noticed, for example, that parent A moved to an inconvenient part of town just so the baby could be with his familiar babysitter each day. "He's used to the babysitter. It would be upsetting to him to move him now," the parent said. Such an attitude reflects wisdom about a child's need for consistency. If a parent has a long-term friend or family member who will be involved with the child for years to come, this is something that will probably benefit the child. It is the child's situation that we care about in our evaluation. A parent says, "I can't help it that I don't have my sweet old mother to watch Deborah every afternoon. It isn't fair that you favor my spouse just because this help is available." Fairness to parents is not the question. From Deborah's point of view, it is beneficial to have this loving, familiar figure care for her each day rather than put her in daycare at a young age. (For the sake of the example, we are assuming that the grandparent is loving and familiar.)

As the child approaches and passes the 18-month mark, his or her needs expand. With the advent of language, the child develops the capacity to objectify himself. This enables the child to experience his or her personhood as something separate from the outside world. It is no coincidence that at about age two, children suddenly begin using the pronouns "I" and "me." The words spoken to them during the next few years will have a shaping influence on how they view themselves in the future. The drive for individualizing is so strong that it creates the typical pushing away, obstinancy, and idiosyncratic behavior that we have come to associate with this period of development. We want the child to be stabilized in the household of the parent who can be at ease with this individuation process. Our interviews and observations have provided a great deal of information on this subject. We noticed, perhaps, that one parent had more of a knack for supporting the child with spontaneously encouraging words than did the other. We liked a parent's laughing attitude of "Okay, do it yourself, big girl!" knowing that this parent would foster the child's growing independence. We were concerned about a parent's resentful and frustrated look when the 30-month-old child shouted "No!" every ten minutes.

The "social" self develops intensively from about age four all the way through the teenage years. A child now learns that the family is not the only place where he or she can find fulfilling experiences. The child has a growing desire to reach out to other adults and to establish peer relationships. We want him or her to be supported in this effort. We favor a parent who will set up social opportunities for the child and will help him or her deal with the interpersonal problems that arise in friendships. We feel concerned if a parent consistently avoids social contact. We see trouble ahead if a parent feels possessive or jealous when the child begins expanding affection to others. We have all encountered individuals who failed to develop the social self adequately. Isolated, shy, or suspicious, they invariably live in private worlds that are too small internally. They lose the benefit of the natural checks and balances that other perspectives provide. Consequently, their ability to cope with new situations or make productive decisions is often impaired. Surveying a parent's own childhood background and looking at the parent's present social network will help the evaluator make good predictions about how these issues will be handled with children.

An important aspect of emotional/social development is the child's feelings about his or her own sexuality. Gender identity is established by the time a child is about two-and-a-half years old. The child will be absorbing cues from both parent about what it means to be a boy or a girl, a man or a woman. Children have a difficult time establishing a stable gender identity unless they have close contact with adults of both sexes. We want to survey each parent's attitudes about sexual issues. How will a parent help the child deal with the issues of sexual awareness that lay ahead? The issues become even more complex as the youngster approaches the teenage years. It is a myth, for example, that a developing teenage girl should live primarily with her mother or an adolescent boy with his father. What an adolescent needs most is to be with a parent who is comfortable with the various feelings and transitions that occur in these years. The parent should exhibit stability regarding his or her own sexuality. The father who at forty is racing around in fast cars and bringing home college coeds for the night may make it difficult for his 16-year-old son to deal with his own sexuality. The mother who is deeply embittered about male relationships may interfere with her daughter's budding trust in boys.

The importance of intellectual development is sometimes neglected by those assessing families. We want the child in our evaluation to have every opportunity to experience all of the gifts of the mind. This issue will start becoming crucial when children reach about seven years old. We will examine the environments each parent has to offer and ask which one best facilitates this aspect of the self. We will look beyond appearances, such as sophisticated books on the shelf, and will inquire more deeply. Father has a nice way of involving his daughter in his activities, such as building cabinets and fixing the carburetor. A girl could learn a lot there. A collateral mentioned that mother sits in a foreign film and whispers the translations to her eight-year-old, even though the audience gives her dirty looks. We wouldn't want to sit next to her, but we commend her for providing this enrichment to her child. How involved is each parent in the child's school work? How attentively does each one answer the child's endless questions? Our collected data help us answer these questions.

In addition to the basic needs that all children have at different stages of life, each child in each evaluation will have specific needs. These should be listed as concretely as possible. Jill is a particularly shy girl, as the evaluator has noted from individual work and from school reports. Which parent seems to "bring her out" more? Which will be attuned to this and help her with it? Donald seems to have a slight developmental problem in coordination and speech. This was observed by the evaluator and confirmed by the doctor. Which parent seems most willing and able to work with the problem? If special therapy is required, which parent will be most supportive of this? Donald's future could depend on how much help he gets.

What will this child's needs be in the future? This is one of the hardest questions an evaluator must address. We are not recommending a living arrangement for next month; we are recommending one for the rest of the child's minor life. The necessity for planning this far ahead continues one of the greatest flaws in the legal system, in the opinion of many mental health professionals. Because children benefit from different experiences at different stages of their lives, a plan enacted today will probably not be appropriate seven years from now. It would make more sense to reevaluate a child's living situation at key stages of development such as at three, seven, and eleven years old. But the court awaits our "Final Recommendation." Consequently, we must strain our vision and look as far ahead as possible. We are not entirely in the dark. We already know what stages of unfolding await our child from a developmental point of view. We realize, for example, that this silent little boy who clings to his equally clinging mother will not always need such tight arms around him. Can this mother let go when he begins to reach school age? Our data about her should help predict this. Our nine-year-old girl has had academic problems throughout her school career. Is there reason to believe that this will suddenly change? Probably not. She therefore needs a lot of time with the parent who will provide the most facilitating environment for her. This will include emotional and academic support.

One prediction can be made with certainty: This child, no matter who he or she is, will need a continuing relationship with both parents. We have reservations about this only if the child has a disturbed or destructive parent, as mentioned earlier, in which case we will want to restrict or monitor contact. If a parent lives far away, we must use our ingenuity to observe this relationship in whatever way possible. Phone calls, letters, big pictures of the absent parent, short and long visits—these will assure that the child maintains a sense of having two parents and experiencing what each has to offer. Someday, the child may choose to live with the now absent mother or father. This option will be available only if we help keep the relationship alive now.

How well and in what ways are Parent A and Parent B able to meet these needs? Having a fairly good handle on the general and specific needs of this child, we ask what each parent has to offer in fulfilling them. Perhaps we make an informal list or chart for ourselves to help organize the material.

Physical Needs

(1) In what ways have the mother and father each demonstrated that they can provide good physical home environments? Among the features to evaluate would be:
   (a) evidence of selecting and creating a safe environment
   (b) evidence of striving to create a comfortable environment that meets the needs of this aged child

(c) evidence of enriching the home environment with aesthetic and stimulating features

(2) In what ways have the mother and father each demonstrated that they can maintain everyday care of the children? Factors to evaluate would include:

(a) evidence of good hygiene and health care

(b) evidence of providing a good diet

(c) evidence of attending to the child's appearance and clothing needs

Emotional/Social Needs

(1) In what ways have the father and mother each demonstrated that they facilitate healthy emotional development in their child? Features to evaluate would include the following:

(a) evidence of giving and receiving love in a manner that the child can experience directly

(b) evidence of recognizing the child as a separate individual with needs and feelings separate from the parent's own

(c) evidence of guiding the child's behavior in a moderate and flexible way

(d) evidence of communicating with the child in a manner that creates openness and trust between them

(e) evidence of serving as a good parental model by attending to their own adult psychological development

(2) In what ways have the father and mother each demonstrated that they can foster the child's social development? Among the factors to evaluate are:

(a) evidence of assisting the child in developing positive social relationships outside of the home

(b) evidence of serving as a good parental model for how to maintain stable, fulfilling relationships

(c) evidence of facilitating the child's ethical development

Intellectual Needs

In what ways has each parent demonstrated that he or she can encourage the child's intellectual development? Among the indications to evaluate are the following:

(1) evidence of providing sensory and intellectual stimulation for the child
(2) evidence of supporting the child in school activities and teaching him or her how to develop intellectual discipline
(3) evidence of providing enriching intellectual experiences outside of the school setting
(4) evidence of functioning as a good parental model by attending to one's own intellectual expansion

In what ways can each parent meet the children's needs in the future? Now we must use our data from the present and the past in order to obtain a reading on the future. If this sounds like we are fortune telling, we should reflect on our overall goal for a moment. In truth, we are making predictions about the future when we recommend a custody plan in our report. The judge is making predictions about the future when he or she issues a custody ruling in court. The prediction is that these children will have the best chance for full development and happiness if placed in certain circumstances. Rather than using a crystal ball, we are using a complex system of knowledge, values, and underlying assumptions. This point will be discussed in further detail later. For now, we acknowledge that our job is to look ahead for the family and see potential developments as clearly as possible.

Having completed our assessment of how the children's needs are met by each parent in the present, we turn to the past. We look carefully at the history of each family member. The children's history is important because it tells us what their physical, emotional, and intellectual experiences have been up until now. If, for example, a three-year-old child has been in the constant care of her maternal grandmother since birth, we know that it will be emotionally traumatic for her to be cut off from that person. If a ten-year-old boy has participated in outdoor activities with his father nearly every weekend since he was little, it will constitute a great loss for him to be denied weekends with the father in the future. Each parent's history is important because it represents the experiential "field" from which the individual operates. The parent's future actions, feelings, and decisions will arise from this context. If a person grew up experiencing the family as a place of safety, warmth, and enjoyment, that person will tend to create these same experiences in his or her own household. Individuals who were slapped repeatedly as children may feel their own hand rising automatically when their youngster misbehaves. Because we as human beings are capable of altering our perspectives and modifying our behavior, we are not slaves to the past. But no one can deny that the past strongly shapes the present and future. These thoughts must sometimes be articulated to parents and attorneys who object when we use past history as a factor in our decision making.

To evaluate a parent's past history, we can quickly survey our list of physical, emotional, and intellectual needs and see how they were met in the parent's own childhood. Was the parent afforded comfortable physical care? Did the parent feel loved in the family? Was open communication facilitated? And so forth. We will not be able to obtain some of the answers. But we will gain a fairly clear overall picture of what we need to know. The parent's history with each child is especially important. This parent is asking for primary custody of the children. Does past behavior suggest that this person can be depended upon to perform the thousand of duties required of a custodian?

It will be noted that the foregoing discussions emphasize parent's strengths and capabilities rather than their weaknesses. This is deliberate. Focusing on a positive attribute gives you something concrete to work with in the evaluation. If, for example, you have observed that a parent is empathetic and affectionate, you can safely predict that a child will feel loved and understood in that household, no matter what other problems may exist. But if the whole analysis focuses on what each parent cannot give and what the child will not get in each home, where does that leave everyone? It is difficult to suggest workable custody and time-sharing arrangements based on a collection of negatives. Second, it should be remembered that everything in the evaluation is leading up to the final report. Parents, attorneys, and judges can use positive information more easily in their own thinking. A negative piece of information is much harder to grasp. If the evaluator says that a child will receive more intellectual stimulation and social enrichment in home A than in home B, the judge can understand that and perceive why it is important. But if the evaluator says that the child will be more impaired intellectually and will experience poorer social development in home B as compared with home A, that is harder to appreciate, somehow. The positive approach also gives the final report a more humanistic cast. Parents are never helped by seeing themselves assassinated on paper.

The Preferences of the Child

Where do the preferences of the child fit into all of this? Everywhere. When a child has indicated that he or she would prefer to live primarily with a certain parent, we put three stars by it in our notes and allow it to have major impact on our decision making. But it belongs to the last stage of the analysis, not the first. We need to understand the family as a whole before we can evaluate its significance properly.

The preferences of the child refers not only to those open, clear statements of choice but also to the less obvious communications we have been given. Our individual work with the children has provided much material about their attachments to each parent. Sometimes they are equally attached to both parents, or, sadly, equally detached from both. More often, though, their emotions lean one way or the other. We observed it in the way they interacted with the parent; we saw that their faces always lit up when talking about that parent; we heard them choose that parent to be on the island with them in the imaginary story; we noted that they felt more understood by that parent. Our question now is, "Is it best for the child to be with the parent of choice?"

Long experience in the custody field tells us that the answer to this question is usually yes. Emotionally healthy children tend to prefer the parent who best meets their physical, emotional, and intellectual needs. Perhaps they cannot verbalize the reasons for their feelings. All they know is that they "feel better" being with that person most of the time. Furthermore, if a child is deeply attached to a parent, that in itself is an emotional need that must be considered. Occasionally, the less able parent was the one who had taken care of the child for many years, and an enduring bond had formed between them. Perhaps the other parent now has more to offer, but the child would be distressed profoundly if forced to make this change. This factor weighs heavily in our decision making.

In many, many cases, our selection of a parent for custodian dovetails nicely with the child's choice. But it is not always that simple. Sometimes, a child's preferences may reflect a temporary rather than a permanent need. The most common example of this is when a child longs for the absent parent. Throughout all of the child's communications, we hear her urgent desire to be with her father. This arises, not because he is meeting her needs better than the mother but because he is failing to meet them (for whatever reasons). Her mother is readily available and their relationship is taken for granted. We as evaluators must be alert to this situation and analyze it properly. Looking at the strengths of each parent and at the past history will help us understand what is really best for the child.

Another misguided reason for choosing a parent is the desire to care for them. This occurs most frequently in children nine and older, but can happen with younger children too. The boy consistently states a preference to live with his mother, for example. Initially we are puzzled by this because in our observation, he has better rapport with his father and seems to be getting more from that environment. Then we begin to see that the boy feels sorry for his mother. He worries about her being alone, and she has played into his sympathy by crying in front of him many times. He feels guilty about being so happy at his father's house. Once we understand this, we can make a recommendation that will really serve the boy's best development. The issue of the needy mother can be addressed through an appropriate time-sharing plan and through a recommendation of counseling for the mother and child.

A third, less commonly encountered reason for gravitating toward the wrong parent is an unhealthy symbiotic relationship between the two. For example, in our evaluation we have not liked what we have seen in the relationship between a parent and child. They seem to bring out the worst in each other, and their history is one of disruption and/or depleting emotional dependency. The other parent seems to offer a somewhat healthier setting. Yet the child prefers the problematic relationship. This is always difficult. If the child is around 12 years or older, it is going to be very hard to force him or her to live in a household under protest. The evaluator may reluctantly recommend that the child's preference be followed, but the report should explain the realities of the case and advocate therapy. As much visitation with the healthier parent as possible should be built into the plan.

In summary, we work hard to understand a child's feelings about custody, and then we examine this information in larger perspective. It is gratifying to find that a child will usually lean toward the situation that is best, as a plant leans toward the light. But unusual circumstances sometimes muddle these instincts. Our job is to sort through these factors and to trust the promptings of our own training and intuitions.

Values, Prejudices, and Biases

When an attorney or parent is not satisfied with a recommenda-tion and cannot successfully attack the evaluator's credentials or methods, he or she can always bring up the values and bias issue. "On what basis did you really make this recommendation? Aren't you operating on a set of private values and forcing them on this unfortunate family? Aren't personal biases operating here?" As annoying as they are, we welcome such questions because they help us clarify our own foundation of decision making.

We have never pretended that we are making custody judgments in a value-free context. How could we? Nothing can be evaluated without using underlying criteria. Even judging a chocolate cake involves a complex set of discriminations and standards. Yet many custody evaluators balk at defining the values and assumptions that shape their recommendations. "Well, each case is so different, and so many factors come into play that no generalizations can be made," they say. It is true that each case presents a unique constel-lation of problems and circumstances. But a core of convictions about "what is good for a child?" guides the evaluator's decisions every time. This may operate unconsciously or at dim awareness. We will take the opposite stance. We will try to understand this core of convictions as explicitly as possible. In this way, we may not always do things right, but at least we will know why we are doing them.

One does not have to look far to find these assumptions. They are mirrored in every statement we make about children and about the impact of parents on children. The evaluation process just dis-cussed is founded on them. Without getting too philosophical, we can summarize a conceptual "stance" that seems appropriate for the work we undertake: Children are predisposed by their biologi-cal natures to undergo certain events that we call "development."

This development does not take place in a vacuum but rather is shaped by environmental circumstances. The family is among the most important of these circumstances. The interaction of all the systems in a child's life can produce an infinite number of outcomes. As evaluators, we are not indifferent about which outcomes will materialize. This is where our values come into play. We have certain preferences about how we want it to turn out for this child. At the heart of it, we want this young person to grow up experiencing satisfaction with life and contributing positively to the lives of others. To do this, we believe that the major aspects of the child's being (which we have characterized as the physical self, the emotional/social self, and the intellectual self) must thrive. But to thrive, the right circumstances are required. What are these? Here we admit a lack of complete knowledge. Human inquiry has addressed itself to this question for thousands of years and the results are still not in. We draw our presumptions from common wisdom, from psychological research, from anthropological knowledge of cultures around the world, and from clinical experience. To discuss them all would require volumes. But the basic tenets are easily identified. We believe that children require consistent and appropriate physical care; that they need the human touch and the love of others; that they must have help in developing language and a positive sense of identity; that they must be enabled to feel connected to others outside of themselves; that they need a context for developing the mind, cultivating self-reflection, and eventually experiencing their own human freedom.

It is unlikely that we would say all of this to the unsuspecting person who asked us about our core assumptions. But mulling it over is useful for our own purposes. Notice that defining our values in terms of a "fully potentialized self" helps us circumvent many cultural biases. For example, an evaluator may not like the fact that a mother from a minority ethnic group plans to have the maternal grandmother rear the child. In the evaluator's cultural background, the mother herself is supposed to rear the child. But will this arrangement foster the child's physical, emotional, and intellectual development? That is the proper question to address. The evaluator may not like that a father is teaching his six-year-old son to defend himself with fists in the neighborhood. But in that setting, will this improve the child's chances to thrive physically, feel good about himself, and adjust to his social milieu? Perhaps so, perhaps not. We cannot know without taking a look at it. The evaluator who devotely goes to church every Sunday may balk at the atheistic mother who "preaches" her beliefs to her child. But this behavior must be evaluated in terms of its impact on the child's development, not in terms of metaphysical precepts. A more difficult situation is the homosexual parent asking for custody. We must not make too many assumptions about the negative effect of homosexuality on the rearing of a child. We will evaluate this parent's ability to foster the child's physical, emotional, and intellectual growth just as we would that of a heterosexual parent. The parent's sexual preferences will naturally have an impact on aspects of the child's social development, and we analyze this in proper perspective. Consulting the latest research in this field will help us here.

Despite our efforts to attend only to the best interests of the children we serve, the challenging attorney's words ring in our ears: "Can you guarantee with 100 percent certainty that no personal biases were operating in your work?" If we say "yes," we trap ourselves, for biases, by their very nature, operate convertly. Those who claim that they have none are the most suspect. Our answer is that we work continually to become aware of our underlying values so that we can examine them. In that way, they lose their power to influence us secretly.

The last point concerning this topic is the most important one. We are not hired as evaluators in spite of our values and assumptions. We are hired because of them. The court correctly assumes that we, as experts, are more highly developed in our ability to judge human situations than is the untrained person. Our long training and experience enable us to handle more complex blocks of information about the families we encounter. Our values concerning children have not been pulled out of the air or parroted from our own upbringing, but are the result of much consultation, reflection, and fine tuning. Our ability to remain steadfastly focused on the needs of the child is one of our most important contributions. For these reasons, we should never fear evaluating our own processes as we undertake the task of evaluating families.

The Final Judgment

Now that all the data have been evaluated in terms of key questions, we should have arrived at some answers. By this point, one parent will have emerged as offering the child the environment that will best facilitate development of the "self." This parent we will recommend for custody; that is, for having primary responsibility in decision making and structuring the child's life. We will provide the youngster with good access to the other parent without disrupting the child's life too drastically. Specific suggestions for accomplishing this are covered in the following chapter.

Our concern here is with "the decision." We use that word knowing full well that the final legal decision is made by the judge (or by the parents, if they settle their own case later). But we are making a decision and we should view it that way. In some cases, the decision is creeping up on us early in the evaluation. We are not alarmed by this, but continue to collect all of the data. We trust ourselves enough not to leap to conclusions. It often happens that a block of new information completely changes the picture for us, particularly if it originates from a child. Other times, the more data we receive, the more our initial suspicions are supported.

Sometimes, though, the case refuses to jell. The facts swirl around and around in the evaluator's mind and sleepless nights may result. It is rare that parents are so equal in their offerings to the children, and the children are so balanced in their feelings toward each parent that the scales will not tip one way or the other. But it does happen. In that case, after much reflection and consultation, the evaluator should abandon the effort to make a custody recommendation and should explain in the report that the children would do equally well in the custody of either parent.

Most of the time, however, there is a problem or obstacle that prevents the case from being resolved. Here are some typical ones for the evaluator to consider in his or her "trouble-shooting" process.

Insufficient Information

Looking over your assessment of how each parent meets the child's physical, emotional, and intellectual needs, are there any major holes in your understanding? Occasionally, an area of importance was just not dealt with in the evaluation. You have no choice but to try to supply this information via another interview or meeting with a child.

You Are Hooked

On rare occasions you may "plug in" emotionally to a case or to one member of a family. This involvement scrambles the signals and makes it difficult to perceive with clarity. A sign of this is that you cannot seem to get a child or adult off of your mind, and there is a definite emotional reaction when you dwell on the situation. It is essential that you consult with another professional in this case. These knots may easily be untangled when speaking out loud to another.

There Is No Good Solution

You look at the case this way and that way, and the options for this child feel terrible no matter what decision you may make. Consequently, no recommendation feels right. Rather than blame your decision-making ability, step back and take another look at the family system as a whole. You may find that it is impaired all the way around and that, indeed, the options are not good for the child. Remember that we are not comparing these two households with other families, but only with each other. Because of the circumstances, we will break our rule of looking for the positive factors (there are not many, right?) and take the opposite approach. Look at both total environments and ask, "Which one will damage the child the least?" Also ask which environment is more open to intervention from the outside (counseling, remedial programs, and so on). Then choose the best of the worst. The final report should reflect the concerns about both households.

You Have Slipped into
a Therapy Role with
this Family

This is a form of getting hooked, but operates at a professional rather than a personal level. It becomes hard to make a decision because you unconsciously see yourself as a helper to the family or to a particular parent. Making a custody recommendation will literally ruin the relationship with one side of the family. You must now reorient your concern back to the children exclusively. It will help to talk to family members and remind them that although some good rapport has taken place between them and you, your job is to make a custody recommendation, even if the outcome makes someone angry. Chances are that the decision will come clear to you after this is done.

You Have Become Too Compulsive

You have already exceeded the number of hours you allotted to this case and have collected mounds of data. But you feel compelled to gather more information before a decision can be made. If the major questions of inquiry have been addressed, you do not need more data. You need to shift away from the particulars and try to see patterns. A good analogy for this is gazing at one of those huge Roman or Byzantine mosaics in a museum. It is easy to get lost in the profusion of tiny tiles so that the picture does not make sense. You also realize that the mosaic is incomplete because some of the pieces are missing and can never be supplied. But if you step back, relax a little, and let the gestalt emerge, the theme suddenly becomes clear. The "theme" of many family interactions can be discerned in just this way. Consulting with another professional is helpful.

Numerous other difficulties often mitigate against arriving at a comfortable resolution in custody. Some cases have no comfortable resolution. We become aware of how difficult it is to wrest answers out of the rubble of divorce. But in all matters of human judgment, we ultimately must fall back on that resource called "wisdom." Cultivating this resource is a life-long endeavor requiring constant personal and professional development. For that reason, the custody field is one in which our apprenticeship never comes to an end.

CONTINUING CASE STUDY
Norcross vs. Norcross

Years ago, a seasoned evaluator said to me, "Don't be alarmed if, in the course of an evaluation, you change your mind two or three times about which party should have custody. This shifting of perspective shows that you are staying open to the various realities of the case. Trust it, and at some point the compass will stabilize, pointing to the right direction."

I have been waiting in vain for the compass to stabilize. In some evaluations, every new fact carries you farther in one particular direction. But the direction here has been a meandering one. It has helped me to put the case aside for a few days and not think about it at all. For me, getting away from the intense presence of the family members helps. Lisa's sad lovely eyes, Angelo's impish little face, Jennifer's strangely magnetic aura, Jacob's endearing genuineness—these rich impressions only distract me from the analytic work that must be done.

My task now is to evaluate the advantages and disadvantages of each environment for Angelo, to assess his attachments and needs, and to try to predict what future course his development would take in each household.

Environments

PHYSICAL ENVIRONMENTS

Looking at the basic necessities of life, both Jennifer and Jacob can be trusted to provide them. They both will feed and clothe Angelo, take him to the doctor and dentist, and will not let the rain run through the roof. But Jennifer offers the child a higher quality physical environment. I was impressed by the way she organized her home, the care with which she maintained the children's room, and the reports from collaterals about how well she dressed the children. Jacob's environment, although adequate, fell far short of these standards. The exception was the yard, which he attended to beautifully. But these are matters of taste and life style. The only feature of Jacob's physical environment that seriously concerns me is his approach—or lack of it—to nutrition. Jennifer's fears about his poor management of food are well-founded. How many ice cream bars would the poor child consume if he lived with the father? What consequence would this have on his health? To be fair, Jacob does seem interested in learning to cook. He could probably be educated about nutrition. But his present blindness about this concerns me.

INTELLECTUAL ENVIRONMENTS

The intellectual advantages of each household are less clear. Jennifer definitely is the more intellectual, academically-oriented of the two parents. She will always have books in the house, will surround herself with intelligent people, and will expose Angelo to enriching cultural experiences. She is correct when she says that she provides an excellent role model in this respect. Jacob cannot measure up to this. But he has two definite strengths to offer. He has shown himself to be deeply concerned with Angelo's education and he would almost certainly remain involved with his schooling. He would be alert to problems that might arise and would do something about them. Jennifer appears to have had only minimal involvement with either children's schools. It concerned me that she never talked to Lisa's teacher about the divorce, for example. Jacob was the one who talked to Angelo's teacher. Because of Jennifer's somewhat self-focused orientation, I also fear that she may tend to gloss over problems that Angelo may have later. But I have no evidence for this so far. Perhaps I am wrong. I think I will approach this subject with her in my next phone call.

The second intellectual advantage that Jacob has to offer is his interest in teaching Angelo. He plugs right into the boy and teaches him all sorts of things. In Jacob's household, Angelo may never hear of Shakespeare, but he will know all about caterpillar tractors and petunias. In the long run, what is more important?

EMOTIONAL/SOCIAL ENVIRONMENTS

The emotional/social factors bring up a tangle of impressions and reactions. Looking at what each parent says about Angelo's emotional needs and how to meet them, Jennifer comes across as the wiser of the two parents. She has read books, attended psychology classes, and had astute conversations about child rearing with her friends. People go to her for advice. Her articulate way of discussing these matters is a joy to hear. Jacob, on the other hand, would be hard put to explain why a child needs a hug.

But "something is rotten in the state of Denmark," to quote Hamlet, as Jennifer herself is fond of doing. Something is very wrong about the way she responds to those kids emotionally. She doesn't seem to connect with them. Except for her serving them food at the lunch table, I did not see her actually interact with the children during the entire home visit.

There was no spark between mother and child, no engagement. Even during the family drawing, which was designed to make them participate together, mother did her own thing. In fact, she discouraged Angelo from messing up her precious roof on the house. She showed no interest in the children's drawings whatever.

More disturbing than this is Jennifer's total failure to read Lisa's feelings. Jennifer told me that Lisa is "losing interest" in seeing Jacob. But in fact, the girl's heart is breaking from missing him. The mother apparently is making no effort to help Lisa maintain a relationship with a side of the family that means the world to her. She does not even seem to recognize Lisa's need, despite all of her professed wisdom about children. Jennifer also conveyed several times that the children had a "wonderful relationship." But the children have serious difficulties with each other. Reports from collaterals support my assessment here. Jennifer said that Angelo wants to live with her rather than with his father. This, too, is incorrect. But this is a more understandable error. Children will often tell both parents that they want to live in their household.

Another issue that concerns me about Jennifer's ability to foster good relationships is her own history. It was a bit chilling to hear her cheerful account of all those broken relationships. She acknowledged that as a child she was able to forget friends right away upon moving to another town. She probably had to assume this attitude in order to protect her feelings. But did these experiences impair her ability to bond

to others? In adulthood, she seemed to abandon relationships with indifference. This included leaving her own child
for three years. Allowing Lisa to live with the grandmother
was not necessarily bad in itself. It was Jennifer's apparent
detachment that strikes me as odd. She never once indicated
that she missed Lisa or worried about the effects of leaving
her. It was Jacob, not the mother, who brought Lisa back to
the family household. Jennifer's romantic movement from
Cliff to Jacob to this new fellow all appeared to occur without
emotional struggle or pain. What are the chances of her staying with this graduate student for more than a year or so?
Who will follow him? What effect will all of these severed attachments have on Angelo?

Looking at Jacob's emotional environment, we see a very
different picture. He comes from a stable background in
which people put much positive energy into their relationships. Angelo would receive a tremendous amount of love
and support not only from father but from the whole extended
family. Jacob himself has demonstrated a good intuitive
grasp of the children's feelings. He anticipated Lisa's emotions much more accurately than did Jennifer. The interaction between him and Angelo was good. Even during the Lego
play, Jacob dovetailed his activities to support those of
Angelo's.

A major emotional/social question is that of separating
Angelo from Lisa. As the mother's petition said, Angelo has
been with Lisa nearly all of his life. At Jacob's house, Angelo
would be spending much time without any other children
around. At Jennifer's home, Angelo could benefit from a
family setting consisting of a mother and sister—a sister
who reads to him and provides companionship. But would
Angelo really benefit from this sibling relationship? My own
observation and those from collaterals suggested that Lisa
harbors hostile and explosive feelings toward Angelo. She is
capable of abusing him. And their mother often does not
seem to notice or intervene. Would these two children do better in a part-time relationship?

Angelo's Attachments and Needs

This issue, at least, is clear to me. Angelo consistently showed a preference for being with his father. During the home visits, Angelo scarcely interacted with his mother. He played with Lisa or withdrew to his room. Not once during the three hours I was there did I observe any physical affection between Angelo and his mother. In fact, they never even had physical contact. How different it was at the father's house. Also, Angelo seemed like a much happier child at his father's house. His face was alive, he laughed, he emitted horrible automobile sounds, and he just enjoyed himself. At his mother's house, his face seemed more devoid of expression, his body movements were quite subdued, and he had a withdrawn quality about him. Mother's statement that he always had eating problems also bothered me. She blamed it on the father, but its cause may originate in her own household.

Angelo's responses in the fantasy stories also indicated a strong desire to be with his father. The only time that he placed himself (or rather his symbolic proxy) with his mother and sister was when they all went out to gather food. How does one interpret this? Perhaps he senses that his mother is more competent in the food department. Also, the way the story was structured, he would go on this journey for only a day, and the family would reunite by the tree in the evening. So going away with her perhaps did not constitute a threat. It suggests that he wants to be with her sometimes, and this is good. But at night, always a scary and insecure time for a little child, he unhesitatingly chose to be with his father in the cave. In the island and truck-family exercises, of course, Angelo also showed a clear preference for his dad.

I felt that the compass needle was stabilizing in the direction of the father. There were disadvantages about his household, but the love, commitment, and stability that he offered were so solid that it seemed to outweigh the other factors. The mother's package had an alluring sparkle to it. But I feared that its center was hollow. But it was time to stop this analysis for now. If my decision was correct, it would still seem correct the next day and the next.

Upon picking up my notes the following day, I began to feel uneasy again. There were so many unanswered questions about Jennifer. What about her relationship with her own mother? Are they close? Lisa suggested that they had had a fight. Why had Lisa not seen more of this woman who reared her for three years? If Jennifer was not awarded custody, based on my recommendation, what would happen? Would she move away, thus depriving Angelo of a mother? If she did get custody, would she support Angelo's relationship with his father? Or would she subtly try to dissolve their bond? She seemed to be doing this with Lisa and Jacob now. But how could I ask her all of these things? It was my job, not hers, to answer many of these questions. She would only give me smooth, well phrased answers, and I would be no clearer than before. But I kept feeling incomplete, as though I didn't yet have enough data. So I called her.

"Ms. Norcross, I am in the process of pulling together the large amount of information from this evaluation. There are a few matters that I would like to discuss further with you. Is this a convenient time to talk?"

"Yes, of course," she said with enthusiasm. "I want you to know how much I personally have benefited from this evaluation. The opportunity to discuss these things with someone like yourself has clarified a lot in my own mind."

I felt that faint flush of good feeling that I had experienced several times before when talking to her. There was something about her. What was it? Why did I respond so positively to this person whom I was planning to recommend against for custody?

"I would like to know more about your mother's role in Angelo's and Lisa's life. We never covered this topic in our discussions. For example, how often do the children see her?

"My mother is the archetypical Grandma, complete with apron and cookies baking in the oven. All children love her. I know I made the right decision in allowing Lisa to spend those first important years with her. Since then, we all see each other when we can. My mother and I are very close. I hope she can come out here for Christmas."

"I am trying to get a sense of how often Lisa has seen her in the last few years."

"Oh, I haven't kept count of the actual number of visits, if that's what you're asking. Quite a few times. Naturally we talk on the phone often."

"I got the feeling that Lisa misses her and longs to see her more often. I think the girl wonders if there is a problem in the family. Is there?

"I'm sure that Lisa would like to have Grandma living in the same house with us. The two of them are naturals together."

Why did I feel that I wasn't getting anywhere with this? Where was I trying to get, anyhow? I decided to change topics.

"I also would like to discuss Angelo's education a little more. Both you and Mr. Norcross have expressed the concern that Angelo might experience a reading disability when he starts school. If it turned out that Angelo did have difficulty, what would your course of action be?"

"Fortunately, the schools are more sophisticated today about dyslexia and other problems. I'm sure they would detect it early and put him in an appropriate remedial program. One of the advantages I can offer Angelo is a household where people read. Children imitate the habits of their parents in this respect. In Jacob's home, I fear the child would never see a book, let alone read one."

Did she answer my question? I couldn't really tell. I took good verbatum notes that I would review later. I asked Jennifer a few more details concerning dates and places, after which I thanked her and said goodbye. Then I sat staring at the telephone, wondering why I had called her in the first place.

The following day, I discovered that I still did not feel resolved about the case. I knew then that it was time to consult with another professional. I called up a colleague experienced in the custody field and borrowed an hour and half of time. I knew I would return the favor at a future date.

I reviewed the basics of my facts, findings, and impressions. I shared my conclusion that the father could probably offer more of significance to Angelo, and that Angelo's deepest attachments were to the father.

"So what's the problem?" my rather tough-mannered colleague asked. (But there was always a great deal of heart behind the "tough.")

"I'm not sure. Details of the case keep swirling around in my head. I'm compelled to look at it this way and that way. That is good to a degree, but usually I resolve things more easily than this. I even made a phone call to the mother that I didn't really have to make. It left me more unsettled than ever."

"It sounds to me like one or both of these parents have hooked you. Or maybe it's the kid. Is this a kid you want to take home with you?"

"No, it's not the children, although my heart went out to Lisa, who has a forlorn quality about her. But her custody isn't in question. I think it's the parents. I think it's the mother."

"Tell me about the mother."

"I find myself thinking very clearly about her when I've been away from her for a few days. But when I talk to her in person, I feel . . . pulled in. I can't put it into words. She's very manipulative and artful. She's . . . "

"She's seductive."

"Seductive! That's the right word. She sort of casts a spell."

"If she can cast a spell on you, imagine what she can do to men."

"You said it! The father fell in love with her five minutes after meeting her."

"Okay, she's hooked you, but what's the hook? You must resonate with her somehow, positively or negatively. Otherwise she would just be another mother in another case."

"I guess there is a subtle identification there in ways. Her aesthetic taste, for example is similar to mine. I nearly

drooled over her Chinese rug, but of course I didn't say anything. Her speech patterns please me a lot. I found myself
talking to her a little longer than was necessary. And at a
deeper level, I guess I feel like being her champion. Here is a
woman of real intelligence, of unusual talent, wasting her life
in a parade of empty relationships. I'd like to see her get her
act together and do something significant. I don't want to
hurt her. And recommending against her for custody will certainly hurt her."

"Will it?"

"Well, that's an interesting question. It will upset her, I'm
sure of that. But is having full-time custody of a wildcat like
Angelo really what she wants? Will it help her further her
goals? I somehow doubt it."

"You know what I think?" my colleague said after a pause.

"What?"

"I think that we can leave this tragic silver-tongued
mother to her own destiny and concentrate on Angelo's
future."

"Good idea," I laughed, feeling somehow relieved. "I
couldn't have said it better myself to myself."

"Now. Let's look ahead for Angelo. Let's assume that his
home base is the father's house. What do you see in his
future?"

"I see him eating a lot of Italian food at the grandparent's
house; I see him playing with his father in the evenings, getting older and replacing his dump trucks with space ships; I
see his father struggling with him over his homework; I see
them living in that same house or one just like it for the next
15 years; I see Jacob getting remarried someday to a woman
not quite as charismatic as Jennifer, but one who gets along
with his folks and maybe likes flowers. Most of all, I see
Angelo feeling loved and secure in the arms of that family."

"And what do you see ahead for Angelo if he lives with his
mother?"

"Hmmm. That's harder. I see him spending most of his time
with Lisa and later with neighborhood friends, because

mother will be dwelling in her own world and will be involved in many activities that don't include him; I see the blond psychology student moving in with them, and perhaps mother marrying him; I see that relationship breaking up and another taking its place; I can't be certain where the mother will live—her pattern from childhood has been to move around a lot; she could take Angelo to another state. Being out of touch with his dad would be a terrible loss for him."

"If you were Angelo, where would you rather live?"

"In spite of all its shortcomings, with Dad."

"I think you have resolved your case."

"I think you are right. And I think talking to you has helped a lot. Thanks."

That afternoon, I jotted down the recommendations and outlined the reasons for them. This would provide the structure for writing the report. I still had to think through the issue of a time-sharing plan. My goal would be to provide Angelo with the best of both parents. Could this be done?

8

Drafting a
Visitation Plan

It is with reluctance that we use the word "visitation" at all. The notion of a child "visiting" a parent seems appropriate only if that parent is in the hospital or jail. Despite its wide use in the court system, many professionals and parents object to the term. It tends to undermine the reality that a family remains a family (but changes form) after divorce. But if we insist on using only our preferred term, "time-sharing," most people will mistakenly believe we are recommending joint custody. In this discussion, therefore, both phrases will be used interchangeably.

After considerable analysis and thought, we have selected one individual as the custodial parent. Our work is far from finished, for we must now draft a set of recommendations concerning time-sharing and other matters. There is also the major question of whether all of the children should follow the same plan. Let us take each issue by turn.

Splitting up Siblings

˙From the beginning, we rejected the idea of "giving" each parent a child based on some misguided concept of justice. In many states, the legal code requires that siblings will not be separated unless there is a good reason for doing so. We adhere to this policy also. Keeping brothers and sisters together under one roof helps them maintain their experience of an intact family. Furthermore, we want all of the children in the family to have the benefit of living primarily in the environment that has the most to offer.

Occasionally, however, we find that siblings should have different living arrangements. This occurs most frequently with older children who may have formed deep attachments to separate parents. The parent-child dynamics may be quite dissimilar for each youngster, and each might benefit by staying in different environments. Sometimes siblings are locked into hostile relationships (which often mirror the relationship between parents) that are serving neither of them. Separating them may be just as wise as separating the parents.

If the evaluator has come to any of these conclusions, individual plans should be drafted for each child. In discussing the time-sharing arrangements, the evaluator should make sure that the siblings have regularly scheduled time with each other. This will help preserve—and perhaps improve—their relationship under new circumstances.

Joint Custody

This is not the place to discuss the merits and disadvantages of joint custody. Opinions range from enthusiastically heralding it as the salvation of the family to discounting it as a fashionable panacea that will create more problems in the long run. Only time, experience, and further research will enable us to assess it properly. As evaluators, our position on it is clear. Unless we are specifically asked to consider joint custody as an option, we will not do so. Parents can always agree to joint custody, even after our report is completed. We should remember that this family was referred to us because they could not settle their differences. They need a plan that will help disentangle them by establishing workable boundaries between the two halves of the family. Recommending joint custody in our evaluations is unlikely to achieve this.

In some instances, we may say in the report that "joint custody would probably work for this family." However, a custody and time-sharing recommendation should still be offered.

Time-Sharing Plans

Our overall goal is to establish the children in the best environmental situation and to perpetuate their relationship with the other household in the most beneficial way. If accomplishing this were as easy as saying the words, drafting a visitation plan would be child's play. But it is one of the most difficult aspects of the whole evaluation.

It is so tempting to throw up our hands and say, "All right, you kids spend half of your time with mother and half of your time with father, and let's be done with it!" Sometimes this plan is appropriate on a temporary basis during the months following the separation. But as a long-term pattern, it has many dangers. Younger children in particular can begin to feel like vagabonds migrating back and forth between households on a daily or weekly basis. Anyone who has ever held two different part-time jobs knows that the mere act of changing locations continually and adjusting to differing environments creates a subtle stress that can be depleting in the long run. It is much more tiring than holding one full-time job. The experience of having a primary residence, which the child has been accustomed to all of his or her life, now is lost. Some children can begin to feel that they truly have two homes; but others never make the adjustment and are left feeling that they have no real home at all. This is especially true if family conflict continues. Practical concerns such as attending school and maintaining continuity in a neighborhood of friends also can become serious problems in a 50-50 time-split situation. In most respects, this plan serves the needs of parents much better than it does those of children. Parents feel that it is "fair," that they "still have" their children. We suspect this to be the origin of its popularity. Children pick up these attitudes also. It is common for a youngster to say, "I like living at my mom's house one week and my dad's house the next week. It's the only fair way to do it." But fair to whom? The growing body of research on visitation arrangements will undoubtedly give us more answers along these lines. Until then, we must base our judgments on what we know about the needs of children. And most evaluators have enough concerns about the possible negative effects of this plan to steer away from it.

What plan is beneficial, then? This will depend on the age and circumstances of the child. Returning to our belief that children need certain environmental inputs at certain stages of development, we can let the age of the child guide our thinking. Such guidelines should not be regarded as fixed rules, but should serve as beginning points for drafting individualized plans.

Birth to 6 Months

By the end of the sixth month of life, most infants will be able to recognize their parents or primary caretakers. If one parent is absent for long periods of time, the infant will probably fail to identify this person as "primary." Therefore we want the baby to have frequent contact with the noncustodian parent. We want the baby to become familiar with the parent's touch, voice, and smell, for these elements are essential for the bonding process to occur. Consequently, the noncustodian should care for the infant actively during their time together. Short, frequent times together are much better than longer visits spaced far apart. From the infants point of view, daily contact of a few hours is ideal. Practical considerations may prevent this from occurring. But the infant should probably not go more than two days in a row without spending time with the noncustodial parent.

6 Months to 18 Months

Intense bonding to the caretaking figures takes place during this period, so we want the noncustodian to continue his or her frequent appearances. Ideally, no more than two or three days should elapse without spending time with the toddler. Sessions of several hours in length suit these children well. Unless the child is accustomed to spending nights away from home base, overnight visits are not regarded as beneficial, even though the noncustodial parent may desire them. Later these overnight visits will be added.

18 to 36 Months Old

With the child's growing ability to conceptualize self and others, the longing for contact with the noncustodial mother or father intensifies. Intimate, communicating time with parents of each sex will serve the development of gender identity and other aspects of psychological growth. As the child approaches three years old, entire days or evenings can profitably be spent away from home base, and overnight stays become appropriate. Entire weekends are often too long for children of this age. Preferably, no more than four or five days should pass before the child sees the noncustodial parent again. A predictable schedule of contacts helps the child organize his or her perception of the world and provides emotional reassurance.

3 to 5 Years Old

Children can make good use of a calendar to solidify their expectations of when the other parent will be with them again. Long weekends, holiday time, and blocks of summer vacation provide enriching experiences. Large photos of the parent and frequent telephone calls help maintain a sense of presence during periods of absence. Children of this age should not be deprived of contact for more than a week at a time, if possible.

5 to 9 Years Old

Due to the development of relationships outside of the family, time-sharing with parents must adapt to school schedules and other activities. The child needs to spend time with both parents, but also desires play time and occasional overnight visits with friends. Many families find that a schedule works well in which the child stays with the noncustodial parent from Friday after school until Sunday evening or Monday morning, every other week. Because two full weeks away from a parent is too long, time during the week after school or in the evening should be spent with the noncustodial parent also. The frequency of these visits should be determined according to the individual circumstances of the family. The noncustodial parent should participate fully in school and extracurricular activities so that the children experience having both a mother and father involved in these aspects of their lives.

10 and Older

Parents may have to step aside at times to accommodate peer relationships during this phase of development. Preadolescent and adolescent children sometimes resist adhering to a time-sharing schedule with a parent. Before the noncustodial parent becomes upset over this, he or she should consider that the child is probably also balking at spending too much time with the custodial parent. As youngsters approach the teenage years, a looser, more flexible pattern of contact tends to work better. Spontaneous weekends, dropping over to the parent's house for supper, making plans for special events or trips out of town—these times together can deepen and sweeten an already close parent-child relationship. Some custodial parents complain that they are in the "drudgery" position during this phase of a child's development, and that they would actually prefer the noncustodial role. In families that are cooperating well together, a wide variety of time-sharing modifications will work. It is not uncommon for a teenager to want to live with the noncustodial parent for a period of time. Because kids need "bigger doses" of a mother or father sometimes, a switch in residence can be beneficial. A healthy family adjusts to the child's changing needs with a minimum of conflict.

Reviewing the above guidelines, we are struck by a certain observation. Children at different ages have different time-sharing needs. Therefore, a fixed visitation schedule enacted when the child is two years old obviously will not be appropriate for the next 16 years. The every-other-weekend plan that courts are fond of ordering can be disastrous for a toddler's relationship with the noncustodial parent. Our goal is to recommend a scheme that changes as the child changes. In general, the periods of contact with the noncustodial parent will be short and frequent when the child is young and will become longer and somewhat less frequent as the youngster grows older. Eventually a more open-ended schedule will be favored. We must spell out such a plan in the report. Although it may seem overly detailed, it can serve the family in the long run. It gives the judge concrete ideas for the final decree. If family relationships improve in the future, the parents will ignore the custody and visitation orders and engineer their own time-sharing plan. This is the best outcome. But if relationships do not improve, at least they have a schedule to follow that will not harm the child.

A final thought concerning time-sharing arrangements may help structure workable plans. Seeing the noncustodial parent frequently during the week, even every day of the week, is not in itself disruptive to children. Unless the families are locked into conflict, this frequent contact can give the child the best of both parents. The disrupting factor appears to be spending too many nights away from a home base. Research results may ultimately disprove this, but at present, clinical experience supports it. Visitation plans that maximize contact with both parents while maintaining a sense of "home base" appear to be the safest. And "home base" means spending most nights in one place.

Holidays

Children should have holiday time with each parent, for the main function of holidays is to reaffirm human bonds. The plan that typically works best is to alternate holidays between parents. That is, the children spend Christmas or Hanukkah with mother this year, with father next year, and so forth. New Years, Easter, Memorial Day, the Fourth of July, Labor Day, and Thanksgiving are the other holidays most often alternated. The child's birthday is sometimes alternated also. Mother's Day and Father's Day are always spent with the appropriate parent. When the noncustodial parent lives far away, this plan must be modified. Children usually cannot take a long trip to spend a one-day holiday with a parent. The long Christmas-New Years holiday can be treated in one of two ways for school children: (a) they can spend the Christmas week (from the first day of school vacation to the day after Christmas) with one parent and spend the New Years week (day after Christmas until the day before school starts) with the other; the next year this rotates; or (b) they can spend the entire two-week period with one parent, alternating every other year.

Summer Vacation

For children over three years old, vacation time with the non-custodial parent is important. This vacation time takes place during the summer in most families. The history, maturity, and circumstances of the child will determine what vacation schedules are appropriate; but we can be guided again by developmental factors. Children of three to five years old are likely to benefit more from several short vacation periods during the summer than by one long one. Three one-week periods spaced over the summer might be suitable, for example. Spacing the time in this manner makes it easier for them to maintain contact with the custodial parent and does not disrupt their continuity as much as an extended stay would. From five to seven years old, two blocks of two or three weeks each tend to work well (for example, two weeks in June and three weeks in August). Children of about eight-years-old and up can spend half of the summer with each parent. Adults sometimes say, "Timothy is with you most of the time for the school year. He should spend the summers with me." But such a plan may not make sense in terms of Timothy's needs, unless he is a mature child and specifically wants to arrange his summers in this way. Youngsters need summer vacation time at their home base also. Little children often have difficulty being away from their familiar home setting and from the custodial parent for that length of time. The transition back can also be hard after staying away for an entire summer. School-children sometimes feel that they have had to give up their circle of friends and neighborhood summer activities, leaving them isolated and out of touch when they return. As one nine-year-old girl said, "I love my (noncustodial) parent, but I wish I didn't have to be gone all summer every summer. I go there in June and feel strange for a little while, then finally get really comfortable there, like I belong there. Then I come back and it feels weird, like I'm this other person with a different name who doesn't belong. None of my friends pay attention to me because they have been doing their own thing all summer. The way it feels is that I am growing up into two different people instead of one."

Voicing such concerns is not to say that spending a whole summer with a parent is always a bad policy. It only reminds us that some of those plans that "look good" from an adult perspective may exact an emotional price for the children who have to live them.

CONTINUING CASE STUDY
Norcross vs. Norcross

I feel at peace with the custody recommendation I am making. Establishing Angelo in his father's home will provide the love and stability he needs. I also trust Jacob's ability to make good decisions for Angelo's future. But without a continuing relationship with his mother, Angelo's development will suffer. How can we provide him with the best of her?

One option is to reverse the present schedule. He could spend the week with his father and each weekend with his mother. But he loses more than he gains this way. It is during the weekends that Jacob and the extended family spend the most time with him. Jennifer, on the other hand, tends to schedule many personal activities into weekends. Her history suggests that weekends have never been "family times" for her. I fear that Angelo would end up with babysitters a lot.

But on weekdays, Jennifer has more flexible time in the after-noons than does Jacob. Why should Angelo be in daycare or at Grandma's each day of the week when he can spend some of the time with mother?

A plan is emerging. If Angelo goes to his mother's house each week at noon on Sunday, he has most of the weekend with his father, but has a portion of it with mother. He then stays at her house Sunday night, Monday, Monday night, and Tuesday until 6:30 after dinner. For portions of Monday and Tuesday, he is in preschool. But mother may be able to pick him up early on both of those days. Leaving Angelo with her Tuesday at dinnertime gives him one more of her good meals. It also ties her in with his school activities rather than relegat-ing her to weekends. He will benefit by this.

This gives Angelo plenty of contact with both households and affords him a nice chunk of time each week with his step-sister. But is it too disruptive? Does it divide up his time too much? I think not. He really spends only two nights away from home base. Tuesday evening through Sunday morning is spent at his father's house. This is much better than those plans where the kids are ferried back and forth every other day between households.

The days I have selected are based on the Norcrosses' present schedules. It is likely that adjustments will have to be made when circumstances change. For example, if mother has a steady commitment each Monday night, it would make more sense for Angelo to stay with her Thursday after school until Saturday at noon. This is the same pattern, moved to a different place in the week.

In two-and-a-half years, when Angelo is seven, this sched-ule may begin to seem disruptive for him. Alternate weekends extending into Monday or even Tuesday may work better at that time. I will recommend that the parents obtain the assist-ance of a counselor or mediator to help them negotiate this schedule if they have problems. But I think that they will be able to work it out on their own, once the dust has settled from the divorce.

Holidays should be alternated between the parents. The mother should have Angelo for this coming Christmas holiday.

Regarding summer vacations, Angelo will be five next summer. I will recommend two vacations with mother of two-and-a-half weeks each. This will give them an opportunity to take a trip if they want to, but will not separate Angelo from his home base for too long at his young age. During the following two summers (he will be six and seven years old), two vacations of three weeks each with mother seem appropriate. That is half of the summer divided into two portions. After that, spending half of the summer (six weeks) with each parent at a stretch seems appropriate. If the mother has moved by then, this summer schedule will still work well.

And Lisa? Although this evaluation is not about her, I cannot ignore her. I will make recommendations even though they may have no legal status. Perhaps Jennifer will pay attention to them. I feel that Lisa should spend at least one weekend a month with Jacob. This will maintain her contact with the only extended family she has now. If the visit takes place on a weekend when Angelo is there, two functions are served. The children have a few more days together each month (under Jacob's good supervision), and Jennifer is afforded one weekend to herself each month. This will be good for her, although that is a secondary concern.

I am tempted to recommend counseling for Jennifer, but I feel it will do no good to put that on paper, and may do harm. She is blocked when it comes to seeing her own problems. She would only feel humiliated by such a recommendation. But if I recommended family counseling for her and the children, there is a chance that she will benefit also. I will emphasize the need for Angelo and Lisa to improve their relationship. It is possible that an astute therapist will work with Jennifer enough to provide some assistance. I plan to emphasize Lisa's need for help in the feedback session with the mother. I wonder whether she will be receptive.

9

Writing the
Final Report

Question: What is wrong with the following paragraph?

"Mr. Walker, father of the child, is a tall, slender man in his late twenties. He appeared for the initial interview neatly dressed in appropriate clothing and seemed relaxed and comfortable. Mr. Walker related a great deal of information about his own family history, his marriage to Ms. Walker, and his reasons for wanting custody of Brad."

Answer: The above paragraph is poor, not because it is badly written, but because it will waste the judge's time with its pointless information. Mr. Walker is a tall, slender man? For whom is that written? The judge can see very well what Mr. Walker looks like, for he is sitting right there in the courtroom. Mr. Walker and Ms. Walker also know what he looks like. He came to the appointment neatly and appropriately dressed? Did we expect him to arrive in his pajamas? And of course he talked about his childhood, marriage, and custody plans. The evaluator asked him about those things.

If you read a dozen custody reports by different evaluators you will find that at least ten of them are padded throughout with unnecessary statements. Our goal is to create a streamlined report that speaks to its audience effectively. To do this, we must be clear (a) what we want to say and (b) to whom we want to say it.

What Do We Want to Say?

Our primary message is that we have arrived at certain custody and visitation recommendations based on assessment of pertinent factors in the case. The factors and our assessment of them are outlined briefly for the court. Nearly every sentence should tie into this message. We say "nearly" because some sentences will serve other functions, such as supporting the parents' feelings.

Beginning with the family history, we select statements that portray the interaction between the parents as it affects the custody issues. We also highlight facts that illuminate the children's experience. Brevity is always the best policy here. The parents met and were married, began having marital difficulties around various issues, separated x number of times, and parted their residences on a permanent basis at such and such a date. Since then, the children have been with the father for these periods of time, and with the mother for these other periods of time. The pattern of visitation has been as follows. End of account. This provides a clear overview of the basic developments in the family without bogging down the reader with a lot of literary details. A belabored history has no place in an efficient report. Why does the judge need to read that the mother once told the father, "When I married you I was still in love with my former boyfriend. I only said yes to your proposal because you were so insistent"? Such details appear in reports regularly. It is not that these facts are unimportant. Some of them may be crucial to the evaluation. But they use up valuable space that should be devoted to an explanation of the evaluator's observations and findings.

Recounting the allegations and concerns of both litigants is another tangle that ensnares report writers. Parents share their fears, accusations, and hopes with such emotional intensity that is is easy for an evaluator to get caught up in them. Consequently, they are allotted too many paragraphs in the final write-up. I have seen reports devote four or five single spaced pages to the parents' allegations. In one document, the writer did such a poor job of organizing the material that it read like an assemblage of unedited case notes. For example,

> During the first interview Mr. Furr said that he thought his wife planned to move in with her boyfriend, Kyle Karsh. This worried the father because he believes that Mr. Karsh does not like the children and will be a bad influence. In the second interview the father added that Mr. Karsh's brother, Ned Karsh, may also live with them. The father related that Ned Karsh has a police record and . . .

In another document, the writer had a flare for capturing the personality-flavor of each parent and included many, many interesting quotes from both of them. Unfortunately, this talent should have been applied to short story writing rather than custody evaluations. For example,

> The mother said that she moved out of the home in April because she could not tolerate the father's behavior any longer. 'I just couldn't take all the fights. He was pickin' on them kids constantly, callin' them little pigs and whores'. . . . Asked why the marriage terminated, the father replied that it was not his idea, but the mother's. Pressed as to why she left, the father replied, 'I think she took a look around her and saw that I wasn't the greatest thing going. I tried to make it up to her. But by then her mind was hung somewhere else."

In all probability, the judge read a few paragraphs of this, sighed, and skipped ahead to the next sections, hoping to find material of greater value.

Remember that in court, the judge will have plenty of opportunity to hear each parent's positions and allegations. The attorneys will probably make opening statements that summarize these. Later, testimony will be presented that fills in the specifics. Nobody depends on the evaluator to elaborate these issues. As was recommended in chapter 2, one succinct paragraph devoted to each parent's position is usually sufficient. Concrete details may be included occasionally if they explain the basis of the allegations. For example,

> Ms. Cooper expressed concern that the father would not be able to care for the children properly if he had custody of them. She related many examples of what she believed to be negligent behavior on his part, including leaving the five-year-old in the car alone while he went shopping, allowing the children go all day without eating, and failing to pick up the children from a neighbor's house until 11:00 p.m. on a school night.

This paragraph summarizes her concerns and the basis for them, but does not squander words on unnecessary details. Neither does it attempt to sort out allegation from fact. It states clearly that these are the mother's statements. Later, other findings will be used to assess the validity of these allegations.

The sections of the report relating the evaluator's data, observations, and impressions are among the most important. These sections are also the most difficult to write. So much material has been collected and so many insights gained that recounting them all might require a ream of paper. We must select the information that pertains most directly to the custody issues and highlights the situation of the children involved. Having done so, we will still be left with too much material to include in the report. We need a structure of some kind that will help us organize our thoughts on paper. Here are three possible structures that may be used:

(1) Discuss each family member in turn, focusing on material that pertains to the custody issues.

The sample report in Chapter 2 uses this model. This is an easy structure because it allows one to present information without having to integrate it into a bigger picture until the final "Conclusions" section. Pertinent findings about the mother, for example, can be discussed in a rather loose way under her heading. These findings generally fall into the following categories: her present living situation (including data from the home visit); her plans for the future and views toward custody and visitation issues (this is different from her allegations towards the other parent); collateral reports about her (friends, employers, and so on); the evaluator's observations of her interaction with the child; the evaluator's impressions of her as a person and parent (particularly as relates to the custody question; that is, one would mention her excellent ability at amateur soccer only if it appeared to enrich the children's lives, or conversely, to take too much time away from them). Information about the father, or other litigant, is presented in the same fashion. Each child has his or her own section. Information about the children is organized around the following issues: data and observations about the child's physical, emotional, and intellectual functioning (evaluator observations and reports from others); the child's feelings about each parent and their environments; observations of the child's interaction with each parent; a summary statement of the child's needs. The "Conclusions" and "Recommendations" follow.

(2) Formulate key questions and then let the evaluation answer them.

This is more difficult to handle, but creates a beautifully integrated and cogent report. The final report in the "Continuing Case Study" is organized in this fashion. After the history and concerns of each parents are treated, a section entitled "Evaluation" begins. It opens with a statement such as, "Based on the information gathered in this evaluation, three central questions emerged as the most critical. These are (a) What does Ethan need in a physical, emotional, and intellectual environment in order to develop in the most beneficial manner? (b) How well does each parent meet these needs? and (c) What are Ethan's feelings concerning his future living situation?" Information and impressions are then organized under each heading. By the time the "Conclusions" section is reached, the conclusion is usually pretty obvious. These are not the only questions that may be used to structure the report. Some cases involve their own central issues (e.g., for a teenager who has overtly stated his preferences, "Is Thomas's stated desire to remain living with his aunt congruent with his best interests?") This approach to structuring the report is particularly suited to visitation evaluations (when custody has already been decided) and modification evaluations (when custody has been legally determined and one party wishes to change it). In the latter case, an opening sentence might be, "In determining what would be in Elaine's and Karen's best interests, it was essential to evaluate (a) the strength and significance of their feelings toward each household and (b) the potential negative and positive consequences of changing their primary residence." Because of space limitations in this manual, neither visitation nor modification evaluations have been discussed.

(3) Using the allegations as a structuring device.

This approach works well in cases that involve serious allegations. Despite our policy of keeping a positive orientation in our reporting, some situations are negative enough to warrant a different treatment. The mother has alleged that the father hits the children with belts, has a serious drinking problem, and cannot hold a job for long. The father alleges that the mother uses and sells cocaine, sleeps around with men, and neglects the children. Our approach will be to take each allegation, compare it against our findings, and evaluate it in terms of the children's welfare. Our findings suggest, for example, that father does use a belt on occasion but mostly threatens the children with such; he appears to have a moderate drinking problem that he acknowledges, and he has agreed to obtain alcohol counseling; he tends to leave jobs before a year has passed but always gets another and does support the family. The mother apparently has used cocaine on occasion but no evidence has emerged that she has ever dealt in it (drugs are the hardest of all allegations to probe); she appears to have intimate relations with numerous men, but not in front of the children, and reports suggest that she makes good babysitting plans for the children when she goes out; she does seem to neglect their diet and health care but gives them warm emotional care. The children's attachments will play a major role in this case. By the end of the report, we will have established a good basis for evaluation which home environment will do the "least damage" to the children. Depending on the severity of the problems, we may recommend that Social Services monitor the family.

It is important to keep the "Conclusions" section as clear and well-honed as possible. It embodies the very heart of the message we are trying to convey. Judges, attorneys, and parents will turn to these closing passages many times to refresh their memories on what the report said. One mistake that new evaluators tend to make is to explain or defend their recommendations much more than is necessary. Their "Conclusions" sections sound like an attorney's closing plea to the court. We do not have to defend the parent that we recommend for custody. We only have to describe the options available to the children and explain why option A will serve their best interests better than option B. If we have presented our information well, we have discussed the strengths of both parents' environments and have probably pointed out areas to be improved. One of the most common criticisms attorneys make of reports is that they "glossed over the bad points about the (recommended) custodial parent and failed to say anything good about the noncustodial parent."

The "Recommendations" section should include recommendations and nothing more. One always has to suppress an impulse to explain things a little more when drafting this part of the report. If an explanation can be accomplished in one sentence, this is acceptable, for example, "Counseling is recommended for Julie to help her deal with her unresolved anger concerning the divorce."

But usually it is wise to restrict oneself to clear, specifically worded recommendations. If the evaluator has explained things properly in the "Conclusions" section, no further discussion should be necessary.

To Whom Are We Speaking?

The writer of the "Mr. Walker is tall and slender" passage made an understandable error. He or she was speaking to an imaginary audience, recounting the circumstances of the interview as a novelist would describe a scene between two characters. We can avoid this confusion by remembering who will be reading the report. Ultimately the report is written for the judge. Even if we feel certain that the case will resolve itself before it goes to court, we should fashion the report as though the judge will use it as evidence. Second, we write for the attorneys. The findings should be explained in a way that will be clear to them. They may disagree vehemently with us, but at least they should understand what we are saying and why. Our third audience will be the parents. Although we are not drafting the report for the litigants specifically, we must always picture them peeking over our shoulders as we write. Often a choice arises between saying something in a negative, potentially injurious way or saying the same thing in more neutral fashion. We choose the second option.

In writing for judges and attorneys, there is one technique that contributes to an effective report more than any other: Don't speak psychologically, speak behaviorally. For our purposes, "behaviorally" refers to describing things in terms of how people act or feel rather than in terms of labels or abstract concepts. For those who have been steeped (too long) in the mental health profession, this advice may be hard to appreciate. The terms we toss around—ego boundaries, borderline personality, individuation, symbiotic relationships—are such common coinage among us that we scarcely notice them. But for most people outside of the field, they can be stumbling blocks to understanding our reasoning. It may take a moments's reflection to find substitutions for our old psychological lingo. But nearly anything can be phrased in terms of behavior or experience. The evaluation has provided a wealth of concrete observations that can be used to make a point. Converting psychological concepts into lay language also works. Sometimes we feel that we have missed nuances in these "translations," but we gain the benefit of really communicating with our listeners. Here are some examples (the original phrases appeared in various custody reports).

OLD PHRASING: Because of the mother's overly symbiotic relationship with the child, there is a danger of her interfering with his individuation process in the future.

SUGGESTED REWRITE: Because the mother has strong needs for keeping the child "one" with her, she is likely to have difficulty allowing him to grow away from her and become his own person in the future.

OLD PHRASING: In the presence of the father, Sondra exhibited regressive behavior which became intrenched as the father's remonstrances increased.

SUGGESTED REWRITE: In the presence of the father, Sondra reverted to acting younger than her age (examples should be inserted here—thumb sucking, whining, and so on). The more the father attempted to correct her behavior, the more strongly she persisted in it.

OLD PHRASING: It was observed that the sibling rivalry between Holly and her sister increased when they were with their father. This had an inhibiting effect on Holly, who became markedly introverted by the end of the session.

SUGGESTED REWRITE: When Holly and her sister were with their father, they bickered, grabbed each other's toys, and competed for their father's attention. This negative interaction eventually overwhelmed Holly, who withdrew to a corner of the room and sucked her thumb.

In each of the rewrites, nonpsychologist readers get a better understanding of what is going on in the family. The final conclusions and recommendations will make more sense to them if they understand the basis on which they were founded.

How do we adapt ourselves to the parents who will be reading the report? We will make two minor modifications, both of which will make a positive difference in the tone of the document. One of them has been touched on earlier—phrasing things in noncondemning and nondestructive language. The "speak behaviorally" rule assists us here. Rather than saying, "The father's rigid, paranoid personality makes it unlikely that he can maintain close relationships with others," we can say, "It appears that the father finds it difficult to trust others and to remain flexible in his everyday dealings with those around him. For this reason, he is likely to have problems maintaining close relationships with others." Notice that the sentence portrays the situation from the standpoint of the experience of the father rather than from an outside critic's perspective. Keeping this perspective in writing can make the harshest of judgments more palatable. Here are more examples:

The mother's psychiatric history and current behavior suggests that she has difficulty distinguishing external events from her own inner fantasies. This makes it difficult for her to respond appropriately to the children's needs and communications.

Information collected in the evaluation suggests that the father has often struck the children with little provocation. He appears to be easily overwhelmed by his own feelings of anger and frustration. For this reason, the stresses of full-time child rearing would probably be difficult for him to handle.

The fact that the mother has changed residences twelve times in the last two years and has lived with at least six different men suggests that she finds it difficult to stabilize her life-style and relationships.

This pattern would create problems for her school-aged child, who needs stability at this period in his development.

The second modification we make for the sake of parents is the addition of paragraphs that are directed entirely at them. Because streamlining the report is always a priority, we can include only a few of these. The feedback session at the end of the evaluation is the real forum for speaking to parents. But litigants read our reports many times. Sometimes a sentence or passage will get through to them, even many months later. Examples of these parent-directed paragraphs are as follows:

The evaluator regretfully found that there was an atmosphere of "armed camps" in this family. Both the mother's relatives and the father's relatives have perpetuated old myths about each other, refused to forgive past injuries, and seemed unable to focus on John's and Kurt's needs. This situation will continue to harm the children if it persists.

One of Jody's primary needs right now is for her parents to cease fighting with each other. Their constant disputes over issues such as the length of her hair, her diet, and her choice of friends is creating intense unhappiness for this girl.

It is hoped that the father will make an effort to devote more time to Jimmy. Throughout this evaluation the child expressed his longing to see his father more often and to feel that his father was interested in the everyday aspects of his life.

Miscellaneous Questions and Answers

How long should the report be?
A good average length for a report is six or seven single-spaced typed pages with spaces in between each paragraph. In cases in-

volving several children or more than two adults, a few more pages may be required. Unless there is an excellent reason for it, no report should exceed 10 pages in length.

When summarizing what parents have said, the wording gets monotonous because we have to say continually, "The mother (or father) reported that" What alternatives are there?

The parent related that . . . ; the parent maintained that . . . ; the parent alleged that . . . ; the parent emphasized that . . . ; the parent recalled that . . . ; the parent felt that . . . ; the parent believed that . . . ; and of course, the parent said that . . ."

Because we don't want to quote children directly except under rare circumstances, what phrasings can be used to convey their feelings?

Here are some concrete examples. When the child has stated a strong desire to be with a particular parent: "Throughout the interviews, Donna expressed her strong feelings of attachment for her (mother/father)." "Robert conveyed his desire to spend most of his time with his (mother/father)." "Janice communicated her feeling of closeness to her (mother/father)." "Daniel shared his fear that he would not be able to continue to live with his (mother/father)." "Cecilia was clear about her longing to be with her (mother/father)." "Ted consistently expressed the hope that he would be able to reside with his (mother/father)."

When the child has not stated a clear preference but has given evidence of strong feelings in one direction or another: "Individual assessment of Sarah suggested that she is strongly attached to her (mother/father)." "Work with Peter indicated that he regards his (mother/father) as his primary source of security." "Mary appears to feel the closest bond with her (mother/father)." "Carl's communications and behavior suggests that living away from his (mother/father) would be very upsetting for him."

What do you say in the "Background" section when each parent has given contradictory accounts of the marital history? Do you relate each of their incongruent statements, or just discuss the facts on which they agree?

Many evaluators get tangled up trying to solve this problem. The worst thing to do is to describe what each parent said. This only muddles the report. You should mention that each parent gave differing and contradictory accounts of the marital history. Details need not be presented unless they concern the living situation of the child. Then the contradictions should briefly be summarized. The rest of the account should focus on facts that are congruent. Here is an example passage:

> The mother and father had been married for about two years when they began having difficulties in their relationship. Each parent gives differing and contradictory accounts of the events surrounding the separation, and these events need not be elaborated here. Of importance is their disagreement about where Deborah lived following the separation. The mother reports that Deborah stayed with her for two months, lived with the paternal grandmother for six weeks, then recently began living with the father. According to the father, Deborah did not live with her mother, but began staying with the paternal grandmother immediately following the separation. Both parties agree that Deborah has been living with her father exclusively since May 14 of this year.

Later in the evaluation, data from other sources can be used to clarify these issues, if it seems important to do so.

In the course of the evaluation, some intimate information about one of the parent's past came to light. To write this into a public document would be embarrassing to the parent. Yet I don't want to leave anything of importance out of the report. Shall I include it?

Details of this nature often emerge during a custody evaluation. The evaluator should ask, "Is this piece of information crucial to the case? Is it a determining factor in the way a parent will rear the child?" If the answer is no or probably not, the information should be omitted from the report. Chances are that the other factors in the case will point to the right custody decision anyway. The report should emphasize these and let the other go by. If the evaluator is asked about this fact on the witness stand, of course, it must be discussed.

In summary, writing a custody evaluation report seems difficult only because it *is* difficult. We must summarize several weeks of intensive analysis into a few pages of words. We must express complicated, convoluted realities in simple, straightforward terms. We must address three distinct audiences simultaneously. When it is finished, we are usually left with the feeling that the report could have been better. Yes, it probably could have been better if we had two extra weeks to polish up the style, or if we had five more years of experience in the custody field, or if the issues in this particular case had been more black and white. As it is, we have the best document we could produce under the circumstances. This feeling of mild discomfort underscores the reality of custody work. We feel unfinished because the human dramas we participate in are unfinished. We experience dissatisfaction because the court system we operate within is not satisfactory for solving these issues. Our skills seem incomplete because each family who touches us will add something else to our storehouse.

Perhaps in the future, we will be able to help families separate and recombine with less trauma. We are beginning to realize that it is useless to cling to old myths about what a family "should be." The traditional "nuclear family" of a momma, papa, and kids under one roof is not the only context for rearing children. Perhaps it is not even the best. As we learn to understand and embrace the new family forms, we will innovate legal structures to accommodate them. Many of the issues that now torment parents, children, and judges will never arise in the new framework. Then, finally, this custody evaluation business will be viewed as a curiosity from the past. And we custody evaluators will regard ourselves as happily obsolete.

CONTINUING CASE STUDY
Norcross vs. Norcross

Even when one is clear about a case's conclusions and the reasons for them, drafting the report feels like a struggle. Should this be included; should that be included? Am I explaining too much or too little? Is the judge understanding my reasoning? But at the end of several hours (always more hours that I allowed for in the fee schedule!), I had a report. My plan was to send the report to the attorneys, then have each parent come in separately to discuss it. Sometimes I arrange to have the feedback session first, and send the report later. But I wanted to give the mother time to read it, have her initial reactions, think about it some more, and then come into my office prepared with questions and reactions. My intuition told me that springing it on her and expecting her to react immediately would be painful for her.

CUSTODY EVALUATION REPORT
re: Norcross vs. Norcross
Court Case No. 314-58740

Evaluator:

Dianne Skafte, M.A.

Participants in this Evaluation:

Angelo Norcross (child in question) d.o.b. 6/6/80
Lisa Norcross (stepsister) d.o.b. 9/30/77
Jennifer Norcross (mother) d.o.b. 11/10/57
Jacob Norcross (father) d.o.b. 5/20/59

Procedures:

At the stipulation of both parties, a custody evaluation was carried out concerning Angelo Norcross, aged four-and-one-half. The parents were interviewed in a joint session and were also seen individually. Home visits were made to each parent's residence at a time when Angelo was present. Angelo was observed in interaction with family members and was also interviewed privately at both households. In addition, telephone interviews were held with the following persons:

—Ms. Betty Burkenstein, Angelo's teacher at Mountain Preschool

—Ms. Marjorie Howard, Lisa's third grade teacher at Baseline Elementary

—Ms. Cindy Fields, babysitter for Angelo and Lisa

—Dr. Michael Davis, the mother's employer at the University Admissions Office

—Mr. Bob Sutton, the father's employer at Star Nursery and Landscaping

—Ms. Doris Byrd, name provided by the mother

—Ms. Rebecca Florien, name provided by the mother

—Mr. Bart Ribe, name provided by the mother

—Ms. Harriet Jankowski, name provided by the father

—Ms. Constance Norcross, name provided by the father

—Mr. John Fernando, name provided by the father

Background

Mr. and Ms. Norcross met in the summer of 1979 when he was 20 years old and she was 22 years old. They married after a courtship of about three months. Angelo was born the following June. Both parents report that the first two years of their marriage was satisfactory, with both of them actively participating in Angelo's care. In the summer of 1981, Lisa, the mother's child from her previous marriage, came to live with the family. The parents reported that Lisa had some problems adjusting to this change because she had lived with her maternal grandmother for three-and-a-half years.

According to both parties, the marital difficulties that began when Angelo was around two years old increased over the next few years. In January of this year, the mother left the household, taking both children with her. After a two-week hiatus when the father did not know where the family was living, Angelo and Lisa began seeing both parents frequently on informal visits. This pattern was disrupted when the mother filed a petition for divorce and custody of Angelo. However, both sides were able to work out a temporary agreement in which Angelo stays with his father from Friday afternoon to Monday afternoon of each week, and with his mother the rest of each week. This schedule has been in effect to date.

It is the mother's position that Angelo's welfare would best be served by living with her. She maintains that she can offer a higher quality of life to the boy. This includes a family setting with a sister whom Angelo has known most of his life. She expressed concern that the father cannot manage the everyday tasks of caring for a child well, especially providing proper meals and nutrition. She also emphasizes that her superior educational level and intellectual aspirations would provide a better context for Angelo's development.

It is the father's position that he can offer Angelo a warmer, more stable family setting than can the mother. He maintains that Angelo would benefit from frequent contact with his extended family, consisting of grandparents, aunts, and uncles. The father expresses concern that Ms. Norcross has had many romantic relationships in the past and will continue to change mates in the future, creating an unstable living situation for Angelo. He also fears that if she had custody of Angelo, she would move away within a year or two and take the child with her. The father said that he plans to continue living in this town indefinitely.

Evaluation

This evaluation centered around two major questions: (a) What can each parent offer Angelo in terms of a physical, emotional/social, and intellectual environment? (b) How can Angelo's needs and attachments best be supported, now and in the future?

The father and his environment offer Angelo clear benefits. Mr. Norcross appears to have excellent relationships with his own family and finds it easy to provide consistent emotional nurturing to Angelo. Throughout the evaluation, Mr. Norcross demonstrated an ability to understand accurately what Angelo and Lisa were feeling. During the structured family interaction, he was able to participate in Angelo's activities in a supportive fashion. Mr. Norcross's ability to relate to children was also noted by a teacher and other collaterals who know him.

Another advantage of the father's environment is its stability. Mr. Norcross has lived in the same town with his extended family most of his life. He has maintained stable employment as a landscaper, and his supervisor commented on his reliability. Based on the information gathered in this evaluation, the father could be expected to provide Angelo with a secure home base into adulthood.

Some aspects of Mr. Norcross's parenting raised concerns. He appears to have difficulty with many practical tasks of managing a household, such as caring for Angelo's clothes and keeping order in his material environment. Mr. Norcross evidences little awareness of a child's nutritional needs. Angelo appears to consume more sugary foods in Mr. Norcross's household than is healthy.

The mother and her environment offer many material and intellectual advantages to Angelo. She has an unusual ability to create a high quality physical setting. The children's room was observed to be attractive and well organized. Ms. Norcross's skills at cooking and attending to the children's nutritional needs were found to be superior. Collateral interviews also supported these observations, noting that the mother has always provided excellent meals and kept the children well dressed while in her care.

As an individual, Ms. Norcross demonstrated a strong commitment to intellectual cultivation. Her lifestyle emphasizes academic development, cultural enrichment, and intellectual companionship. This could benefit Angelo by providing exposure to these values. In later years, when his mind and interests are more mature, her contribution could be particularly valuable.

Of concern is the mother's difficulty in understanding the feelings of her children. She has failed to perceive, for example, that Lisa is experiencing much pain over the loss of her stepfather and longs to spend more time with him. Ms. Norcross apparently has done little to help the girl with her feelings about the separation. Assessment suggests that the mother has problems establishing warm emotional connections with Angelo and Lisa. Her own history of numerous severed relationships raises concerns about her ability to maintain close, long-term commitments.

ANGELO'S NEEDS AND ATTACHMENTS

Throughout the evaluation, Angelo's behavior and verbalizations indicated that he feels happiest and most secure in the presence of his father. During the home visits, he came across as more cheerful, spontaneous, and cooperative when with his father than when with his mother. Fantasy play consistently favored his father's home as the place he preferred to be. In addition, the interaction between Angelo and his father was assessed to be much more affectionate and communicating than was the interaction between Angelo and his mother.

Conclusions

It is clear that each parent offers Angelo certain benefits and presents certain problems. The goal of this evaluation is to recommend a living situation for Angelo that will maximize his physical, emotional, and intellectual development in both environments.

The information gathered in this study suggests that Angelo will find a more secure, nurturing home base at his father's house. It appears to offer a more consistent and understanding family setting than does the alternative environment. Furthermore, Angelo's strong desire to be with his father cannot be ignored. All indications suggest that his strong feelings of attachment for Mr. Norcross are based on a positive, satisfying past relationship with him. To separate the child from this relationship now would create much emotional distress for him.

Mr. Norcross's previously discussed shortcomings as a parent are ones that could be improved through education and awareness. Adult education courses in nutrition, cooking, and household management would benefit him and Angelo greatly. Though his family constitutes a positive influence, he would do well to depend on them less and acquire more needed skills on his own.

Angelo's mother provides him with benefits that are crucial to his development and cannot be replaced. It is felt that she can contribute to his life most effectively in the noncustodial parent role. The intelligence, enrichment, and creativity that she embodies can be provided to Angelo as long as they have adequate time together.

The relationship between Angelo and Lisa should be protected. Although they have problems, they are important to each other. The recommended time-sharing plan is designed to foster this relationship. The mother is advised to obtain family counseling during this period of adjustment for the children. An improvement in their interaction would benefit both households.

Lisa's custody is not in question, but she is an integral part of this family. It is important to her psychological well-being that she maintains contact with her stepfather and his family. Mr. Norcross has expressed his desire for continuing this relationship. Therefore, it is recommended that Lisa spend at least one weekend a month with him at a time when Angelo is there. Spontaneous visits after school or on special occasions are also supported if it does not create conflict between the parents.

Recommendations

   (1) That Angelo be placed in the custody of his father.
   (2) Than Angelo spend three days and two nights with his mother each week. The following schedule is sug-

gested, although changing circumstances may dictate an adjustment: Angelo goes to his mother's house each Sunday at noon and stays until Tuesday 6:30, after dinner. She takes him to school and picks him up from school each Monday and Tuesday.

(3) That Angelo's time-sharing schedule be reevaluated when he reaches the age of seven. Alternate weekends extending to Monday or Tuesday with his mother may be more appropriate. It is suggested that a mediator or family counselor assist the parents in arranging this schedule.

(4) That holidays be alternated between the parents, and that Angelo spend the first Christmas with the noncustodial parent.

(5) That Angelo spend summer vacation time with his mother as follows:
   (a) This coming summer, two separate vacations of two-and-a-half weeks each
   (b) The following two summers, two separate vacations of three weeks each
   (c) Each summer thereafter, six continuous weeks (half the summer)

(6) That the father participate in classes or training to improve his domestic skills

(7) That the mother participate in family counseling to improve the relationship between Angelo and Lisa

POSTSCRIPT:
Norcross vs. Norcross

I scheduled the final "feedback sessions" with each parent separately. I had considered seeing them together, but that would have inhibited them in different ways. Jacob never expressed himself well in front of Jennifer. And Jennifer would not want Jacob to see how upset she was about the custody outcome. She might come across as sarcastic or cooly confident, and this would not serve any useful purpose.

Jacob came to his session all flustered, not knowing whether to feel elated, awed, sorry for Jennifer, or all three at once. I told him that there was no need to feel any of those things. Nobody was winning or losing here, despite how attorneys might view it. We had a little boy who needed both of his parents, but who also needed the stability of a home base. I felt strongly that the recommendations would afford Angelo the best of both households. Whether anyone else agreed with me remained to be seen.

I asked Jacob how he felt about my recommendations to go to a few classes on household management. He grinned and pulled out a summer schedule from the Community Extension School. He had signed up for an evening cooking class that started in three weeks. Classes in housekeeping probably were not available, but he had heard of a program through Social Services that he was going to investigate. I sensed that Jacob was really excited about all of this. That willingness to learn and to use the assistance of others was one of his most important strengths, I felt. It would serve Angelo in the long run. I had forgotten to mention that in the report. Oh well.

We spent the rest of the time talking about the children and what they needed from each parent. I explained in detail Lisa's feelings about missing him and the grandparents. Jacob's eyes filled with tears when he heard this. He told me that he loved that girl and would do all he could to let her know it.

For some reason I felt a little nervous about the impending session with Jennifer. It is always more difficult to face the parent who was not favored in the report. The person is invariably angry, defensive, or crestfallen. My personal "hook-in" to Jennifer was operating too, I was sure. So I took a deep breath and greeted her in the waiting room.

Her sunny smile, her warmth, her arresting gaze had all vanished. The eyes that regarded mine were as cold as steel.

We sat down in my office and waited for each other to speak. I saw that her copy of the report was marked heavily in red pen with comments, exclamation marks, and arrows.

"Judging from that," I gestured toward the report, "I am guessing that you are not pleased with the evaluation."

"Did you expect me to be?"

"I didn't know how you would feel. Would you like to discuss it?"

"Is there a point to discussing it? You aren't prepared to change your mind, I take it."

"I feel that the recommendations in the report will give Angelo the best of both of his parents. That was my only objective."

"Well I think you made a colossal error in judgment."

"Yes, I see that you do."

"You completely misinterpreted everything I said. You based your impressions of our relationship on that home visit. Just because Angelo didn't slobber in my arms you assumed that we weren't affectionate. Who the hell are you to say that I don't love my son?"

"Who said that you don't love your son?"

"The report as much as said it. It is the most humiliating document I have ever read."

"Tell me what is humiliating."

"To lose custody of my child is humiliating! Do you now how that looks? What am I, some kind of an unfit mother? And to recommend that boob for custody—I had no idea it would turn out like this. I should never, never have agreed to this evaluation."

"The pain for me in all of this is that someone had to feel like they have lost. The present court structure does this to us. But Angelo hasn't lost anything, has he? The recommendation suggests that he see you three days a week and see his dad four days a week. That really isn't very different from the way things are now for him."

"Except that I lose custody of my child."

I could see that Jennifer was not able to look at things from Angelo's point of view, at least not now. She was smarting under the impact of what this meant for her personally. I had compassion for this. But her reaction only supported my original assessment: that her own feelings and needs had much more reality and priority than did those of her children.

Jennifer was not pleased with the direction of the conversation. As always with these evaluations, I was in a difficult position. I could not function as a therapist to help her vent all of her anger and frustration, because I was the cause of much of it. Yet it was too coldhearted simply to say, "We are here to discuss specific points of the evaluation and nothing more. Therefore you will kindly keep your feelings to yourself." My approach was to try to strike a balance that would touch on her feelings but also focus on Angelo's welfare. Perhaps I failed at both endeavors.

I heard nothing more about the case for three weeks. Sometimes the attorneys call with questions, comments, or condemnations.

But neither Gomez nor Chappel contacted me. I assumed that the matter would go to court and that I would receive a subpeona from Gomez one of these days. (Because I had recommended custody for her client, she would call me as her witness.) But I was wrong.

On Thursday Ms. Gomez contacted me. She said that the case was not going to court because the couple had worked out an agreement. They decided to have joint custody, with each of them participating equally in making decisions for Angelo's life. They agreed to follow the time-sharing plan exactly as I had recommended it. Ms Gomez related that she had talked to Jacob for hours trying to dissuade him from agreeing to joint custody. She said that he was opening the door for all sorts of problems later on. But he could not be convinced. He said that Jennifer loved Angelo as much as he did and should be able to call herself a custodial parent also. He felt that someday Angelo would like it if his parents had joint custody agreement. She asked me how I thought this plan would work.

I told her that it probably had a good chance of working, particularly if the couple sought mediation or counseling when things got difficult. I did not anticipate them having problems over major issues such as religious training or the choice of schools for Angelo. The most important thing was that they had a good time-sharing plan for Angelo; and naturally I thought the one they selected was good. If they had intended to leave it open-ended or have him bouncing back and forth at random, then I really would worry. The main problem I can see in the future is that if the mother wants to move away and take Angelo, the father will not permit it. Because neither of them has the legal power to decide this, they will probably end up in court.

"We already took care of that," Ms. Gomez said. "They agreed that if either parent wanted to move more than 75 miles away, that Angelo would stay with the parent living here. Because Jacob will probably remain in this town until he is 87 years old, the agreement favors him. I'm not certain that it would hold up in court, but it may discourage the mother from trying to move to the other end of the country with Angelo.

"That was an excellent idea," I commented. "Angelo will do best with both parents living near him."

"It was Jacob's idea, did you know that? I must say that he really surprised me during this custody dispute. On the surface he doesn't come across as very smart. But underneath there is a well of natural wisdom."

"I agree," I said. "It reminds me of something he said during the evaluation."

"What was that?"

"Some of the plainest plants have the most beautiful root systems."

About the Author

Dianne Skafte is a private practitioner in individual and family counseling in Boulder, Colorado. In addition to her role as a therapist, she specializes in custody evaluations and custody mediation. She is Custody Evaluator with the Child Custody Assessment Team, and has worked in that capacity with the Dallas County Probation Department and the Boulder County Department of Social Services. She has written many works in the field of child custody and has presented workshops and lectures in the field.